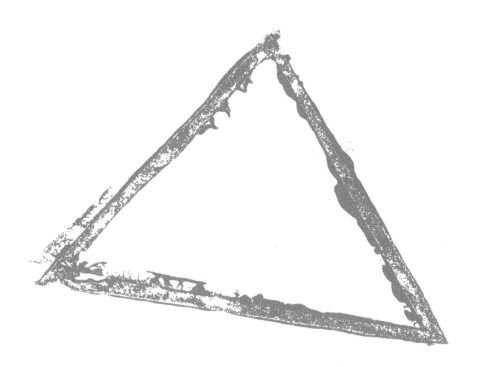

Other Books by Mike Ricksecker:

A Walk In The Shadows: A Complete Guide To Shadow People

Campfire Tales: Midwest

Ghostorian Case Files: Volume 1

Ghosts and Legends of Oklahoma

Ghosts of Maryland

System of the Dead

Deadly Heirs

Encounters With The Paranormal: Vol. 1-4

ALASKA'S
Mysterious
TRIANGLE

Mike
RICKSECKER

First Edition:
First printing

PUBLISHED BY HAUNTED ROAD MEDIA, LLC
www.hauntedroadmedia.com

Cleveland, Ohio
United States of America

To my grandfather, Grant Ricksecker:
I know somewhere you have a map out on a table and are
following these adventures. I miss you.

ACKNOWLEDGMENTS

The very first acknowledgment I need to make in this book is to my best friend in high school, Ron Stevens. If not for him, I would never have enlisted in the Air Force to begin with and set myself on the path I am on today. Without writing out my complete autobiography, it was through his persuasion that on September 27, 1991, I signed on the dotted line. By the middle of June after my high school graduation the following year, I was in basic training, and by November 1992 I was exiting the flight that landed me in Alaska. While he did try to talk me back out of it before I left for basic, I stuck by my decision and started my adventure, one that I would never even have thought of considering if he hadn't proposed the idea to me in the first place. I must thank you, my friend.

I also need to thank Mike Parkes and the crew at Wild Dream Films in the UK for reaching out to me about the opportunity to be a part of *The Alaska Triangle* television show. It's been amazing to dive headlong into these topics that I just heard whispers about while I was stationed at Elmendorf AFB, and to have an opportunity to re-examine my own experiences that occurred more than (as of this writing) a quarter of a century ago. All these years later, to go back and explore a place where I spent three years of my young adulthood through much more seasoned and experienced eyes was quite surreal. Mike and Wild Dream were all completely a class act, and I thoroughly enjoyed working with them.

Jonny Enoch and I became fast friends through our connection and appearances on *The Alaska Triangle* (again, thanks Wild Dream), and we've had several other adventures together since then, including an amazing excursion to Egypt. Jonny has written the foreword to this book, but he's also helped encourage me along the way to get this work completed. So, while I must thank my friend for his support through this, I must also thank the phenomena in the Alaska Triangle for connecting me with my cheeky Moravian brother.

Another fast friend I met through this experience was Jeremy Ray of MUFON. Jeremy has to be one of the most likable and down-to-earth guys in the world, and I was thrilled to have met another one of my *Alaska Triangle* brethren at the UFO MegaCon in June 2021. Thank you for all the positivity, my friend.

A quick thanks to David Weatherly and his book *Monsters of the Last Frontier*. Cryptids aren't my strong suit – there's a *ton* of material on the subject matter – but my friend provided some fantastic insight in this department.

There are too many friends and family to list here that have had some hand in this Alaska experience over the years. Who all do you thank for things that happened a half a lifetime ago and how many people are there to thank for the adventure that's happening now? Countless. My parents have always been supportive of anything I've done (even when it's been absolutely bonkers), so I must always thank them, because without them I do not have the foundation of who I am today.

While they missed me and I missed them, so many people

helped to make me feel comfortable my first few years away from home living thousands of miles away. I still have the little Christmas tree my parents shipped to me that first winter. My sister sent me nearly a card a week for a while. My friend, Amy, got a group of her friends to bake me cookies, and they shipped them up inside a box full of popcorn. My Aunt Marge got the kids in her class to write me a bunch of letters. Several of my high school classmates became pen pals, and we kept in touch that way for a while until email came along. Family that trekked up to Alaska during those years included my grandparents, my Uncle Chuck, my Aunt Marge, my mother, and my sister. I thank them all *immensely* for that. (My dad wasn't able to make the journey northward since he and my mom were breaking ground on the new house they were building, and I still bust his balls on occasion for not putting off the groundbreaking a week or two.)

I must thank all of the supporters I've had throughout the years who have been reading my books, following Haunted Road Media, and most recently have become a part of the experience at the Connected Universe Portal. Without all of you, none of these continued adventures would even be possible. You are all amazing!

And, of course, I must also thank my partner, Nicole Antoinette Guillaume, who has been an absolutely amazing support and inspiration throughout this whole process even while I sequestered myself in the studio for a month to complete the last parts of this book. Standing by me with your unwavering love means the world to me!

TABLE of CONTENTS

Jonny Enoch

FOREWORD

The Alaska Triangle is one of the most frightening and mysterious places on earth. Not only does it have 33,000 miles of coast and 3 million lakes, but more than 16,000 people have disappeared without a trace over the last 30 years. We also find legends of giants, elongated skulls, big foot, and underwater UFO bases. Alaska was no doubt connected to a lost ancient civilization like the Atlanteans, as it has been suggested that there is a massive coverup concerning an underground pyramid there.

Much like the Bermuda Triangle, the Alaska Triangle is surrounded by energy vortices that have caused planes to vanish and act like portals to other dimensions. Mike Ricksecker has done an incredible job of collecting stories from around Alaska, interviewing witnesses of strange phenomena, and measuring energetic fields there.

Having co-starred with him on the Travel Channel's *The Alaska Triangle* and exploring Egypt together, I got to witness his never-ending pursuit of uncovering the truth about these great mysteries. In my opinion, this book is the most thorough investigation that has ever been done on this subject and is an invaluable resource for anyone who has ever lived in Alaska or wanted to visit and explore its mysteries. As you turn the pages of this book, you will be shocked by what you read, and you will never be the same again.

Jonny Enoch
Host on Gaia TV

INTRODUCTION

It was only November 1, 1992, when I stepped off the airplane into a bitter chill and discovered several inches of snow and ice already piled on the frozen tundra. The sky had long fallen into darkness, so I couldn't see the looming, snow-covered mountains that engulfed the city of Anchorage, but Alaska had already greeted me with its icy kiss. That kiss would linger upon me throughout a three year tour at Elmendorf Air Force Base until I departed on the same date in 1995, eventually returning twenty-four years later in May 2019 for filming of the Travel Channel series *The Alaska Triangle*.

The television show focused on strange phenomena that occurs in a massive stretch of land that reaches from Juneau, to Anchorage, to Utqiagvik (formerly Barrow), including missing persons, airplanes, and ships, UFO sightings, hauntings, Bigfoot reports, and more. This is an area of the world in which more than 16,000 people have gone missing since 1988 at a rate that far exceeds the national average. Experts from around the world like Jonny Enoch, Hugh Newman, Jeremy Ray, Andrew Gough, Cliff Barackman, and more were brought in to weigh in on these phenomena, some trekking out into the depths of the wilderness.

These men are amazing, and have been researching these types of strange occurrences for decades, as have I. What made me a little different, however, is that other than the locals who were interviewed for the show, I had actually previously lived in Alaska and experienced the Triangle's strangeness first-hand.

I was a brand-new Air Force recruit when I stepped off that airplane in 1992, fresh out of training in the sweltering summer heat of Texas and Mississippi. I had graduated high school just months beforehand, and only 14 days after tossing my cap into the air with my classmates I found myself donning a camouflaged hat at Lackland Air Force Base in San Antonio and marching – incessantly marching. Now, in Alaska, instead of sweating bullets I'd be freezing my assets.

What wasn't really noticeable until dawn the next morning was that the small, light flakes gently falling from the sky weren't completely white. There was a bit of gray mixed in with them as well, and my sponsor, John, told me of the recent volcanic eruptions of Mt. Spurr across Cook Inlet from Anchorage and Elmendorf where I was stationed. Sure enough, for the first several weeks of my tour we covered computer equipment at the end of the day so the ash wouldn't settle on the electronics at night. In fact, when I bought a truck several weeks later and opened the hood, there were piles of ash around the interior lip. I'd come to learn these were "only in Alaska" type moments.

Not only would I experience my first volcano fallout within those first few weeks, but I would also experience my first earthquake. I couldn't tell you the magnitude; I just remember standing near my workstation and talking with a few of the other airmen when, all of a sudden, the floor started to move as if it were on some sort of wave machine. I reached out to grab a hold of a cubicle partition to steady myself, but much to my dismay, this did no good. One of the guys said, "The earth is moving. There's not much you can do about it."

At Chugach State Park in spring 1993.

Months later, we were rocked with a 6.9 magnitude quake that sounded like a cannon went off nearby. I remember it clearly. I hadn't been asleep long in bed in my dorm room when, what I at first thought was an explosion, blasted the complex. I was at an Air Force base not all that far from what had only just recently been the former U.S.S.R., so instinctively, who knew what could truly be happening. I shot up in bed and everything started shaking, violently. The room pitched, lurching to the left, and that's when I realized it was an earthquake. I wasn't kidding on *The Alaska Triangle* television show when I said the land was volatile. Everything finally settled, and my then-girlfriend (soon to be wife, later to be ex-wife) called crying from miles away in Eagle River. Also, in the Air Force, she was from California and had experienced numerous earthquakes before, but this one had scared her. Only in Alaska.

To be honest, I did not really care for living in Alaska while I was there, although my grandfather (to whom this book is dedicated) loved it when he visited with my grandmother and my aunt and uncle the first summer I was stationed there. I was young and homesick during those years, and the long, bitter-cold winters can seriously wear on the psyche, especially with how soon it grows dark during the winters (I primarily worked in the secured basement of the ALCOM (Alaska Command) building ... if I didn't go outside for lunch, I didn't see sunlight that day). The running joke amongst the military personnel was that when you get stationed in Alaska you either get married, have a bunch of kids, get divorced, or do all three. I managed two of the three while there. That said, it's an amazingly beautiful place to visit, and I now have a ton of colorful stories from there to tell.

For instance, there was one night when my then-wife picked me up from a second job I was working (when you're a young, low-ranking airman, married, and with children, you need all the extra income you can get), and she was simply driving us down Debarr Road which is a main drag that feeds the east side of town into downtown Anchorage. It was winter, but the road was well-lit, and even though it was a fairly-well populated part of town there was a moose standing in the middle of the road up ahead. My ex was going on talking about whatever she was talking about, and we were getting closer and closer to the moose just standing in the lane. Even with the decent lighting, she apparently didn't see the large mass of fur and antlers and was just cruising along until, finally, I pointed up ahead and said, "Are you going to try to miss the moose?"

At that, she finally noticed the animal, screamed, and slammed on the brakes. There's no such thing as a dry road in the winter in Alaska, so she spun out on the ice 180 degrees into a snowbank on the righthand side of the road. The moose tore off into the trees never to be seen by us again. Once again, only in Alaska.

Speaking of winter driving, I believe everyone should spend a winter in Alaska learning how to drive in those kinds of conditions and weather. Most people down here in the "Lower 48" have no clue what they're doing on the roads when snow and ice hit the region, but in Alaska you have no choice but to learn. Those three years were an intense crash course in winter weather driving – so, I've got that going for me.

I experienced my first real tastes of skiing and snowboarding in Alaska, had half my children up there, played my last organized baseball in an Anchorage league, viewed countless beautiful vistas of the Aurora Borealis during the winters, can say I went shirtless in 30 below-zero temperatures (not recommended), experienced ice fog, battled through the then-third most ever snowfall recorded in a season in Anchorage (121.5 inches), and observed one of the most beautiful things I've ever seen on the drive out. Yes, following a snow storm for days, on November 1, 1995, we *drove* out of Alaska. On the second night, before we caught back up to the storm, we crested a ridge on some mountain range (I couldn't tell you which ... we were likely lost, and I have no idea how we survived given our young age and the fact we drove this in a freaking Geo Prizm), and there in the valley with the moonlight glimmering off the new-fallen snow was a herd of caribou covering the road. I slowed down and soaked it in. It looked just like a postcard or some image a filmmaker shoots for a Christmas special ... except this was real. I wasn't sure how we were going to get the car through given the size of the herd, but I carefully inched toward them and, to my amazement, they simply parted like water. It was insanely beautiful. To me, that moment was a gift from the universe for the three years I'd spent in the frigid far north.

Twenty-four years later, Wild Dream Films flew me back into Anchorage to film *The Alaska Triangle* for the Travel Channel. The area known as the Alaska Triangle, much like the Bermuda Triangle, is known for its anomalous activity, as previously mentioned, and I'd certainly seen my share of it in the years I'd spent living there. My ex-wife and I even believed our first apartment together had been haunted, and the second, while we debunked what we originally thought may have been paranormal activity, still had an extremely creepy vibe to it. But that's not what my appearances on the show were about.

The Alaska Triangle *reunion at the Laughlin UFO MegaCon 2021. This motley crew includes, left to right: Jeremy Ray, Mike Ricksecker, Jonny Enoch*

My appearances on *The Alaska Triangle* in the episodes "The Missing Douglas," "The Alaskan Titanic," and "Alaskan Bigfoot" (the "Mysterious Forcefields of the Triangle" segment) were to talk about portals and vortices and how they affect the region. This has been a growing part of my research of the connected universe and how these supernatural forces affect us all. Or are they really supernatural? Renowned paranormal researcher Dr. Hans Holzer used to say, "There's no 'supernatural world.' Everything that exists is natural." Can a natural vortex open a portal into another dimension? That's something that was postulated on *The Alaska Triangle* television show, and it may very well be true. The ancients used to tap into the telluric currents of the Earth, using its energy for a variety of reasons, including entering altered states of consciousness, healing, and more. Opening a doorway into another dimension could very well be another one of those reasons.

The human body is an aggregate of an energy field, and that field is interconnected to everything that exists. Energy is the unique engine that drives everything including our consciousness, and as such, energy can influence us and we can influence it. This energy field is a force and it is full of information, or as Einstein succinctly stated, 'the field is the only reality.'
(Silva, Freddy. *The Divine Blueprint*, p. 229.)

There's definitely something strange and mysterious about this triangle area of Alaska, and further research may help reveal answers to, not only mysteries of the Alaska Triangle, but perhaps, to other locations around the world that exhibit similar activity. Each chapter within this volume really could have an entire book written about the subject. One day on the side of a mountain with a couple of dowsing rods is really just an introduction to what may be going on in the great white north, the very, very tip of the iceberg (pun intended). We'll continue to explore the possibilities of vortices, portals, and other dimensions as we move forward, not only in this book but in the others that follow. The Alaska Triangle has just been one stop of many along the journey ... but let's pull on our parkas and mukluks and examine it while we're here.

Chapter 1

COLD LESSONS IN TRIANGLES, VORTICES, AND PORTALS

The twilight glittered across the vast expanse of the evening sky, the stars in their infancy bursting forth from the womb of space. Languid waters surrounding the three westward sailing ships reflected the heavens like glass, a silky purple speckled with pinpricks of twinkling white lights, almost as if the ocean was filled with tiny swimming fairies. The little shining ones could have sung their lullaby and gently rocked the crews to sleep had not the twilight tore open in a white-hot blaze, sizzling and crackling as the heavens suddenly hurtled toward the Earth. Wide-eyed men gazed up and clamored toward the edges of their respective decks, pushing, shoving, and jostling for position, mouths agape as they witnessed the flames plummet into the ocean several leagues away. The admiral's log would describe the phenomenon that night as a "marvelous sheet of fire" that fell from the sky, but the entry would later become known as one of the first documented marvels of the Bermuda Triangle – and that admiral guiding the vessels was Christopher Columbus in 1492.

The 500,000 square mile swathe of ocean stretching from what we now call the island of Bermuda to Miami, Florida, to Puerto Rico is, perhaps, the most enigmatic area of water on the planet, rife with strange phenomena and mysterious disappearances. Columbus also experienced erratic compass readings in the triangle area and observed strange lights that he described as like "a small wax candle being raised and lowered" in the night sky, but it wasn't until 1918 when the *USS Cyclops* and its crew of 309 went missing in these waters that the legends of the Bermuda Triangle really started to take shape. There had always been a bevy of shipwrecks around Bermuda due to its shallow shoals, but as technology became better, losing an entire ship and its crew with no word whatsoever became extremely suspect, and observers began connecting the dots with other strange occurrences in the area. It was odd, perhaps just a coincidence, during World War II when the two sister ships of the *USS Cyclops* also went missing (albeit, in the North Atlantic), but when five torpedo bombers known as Flight 19 completely disappeared in the triangle in 1945 and then one of its search and rescue planes also disappeared without a trace, the Bermuda Triangle grew to legendary status and has now become the subject of countless books, movies, and television shows. It's also become the inspiration for naming all other areas around the world that experience similar strange phenomena a "triangle," including the Alaska Triangle, which has also been called at times "Alaska's Bermuda Triangle."

One could spin the globe and find a number of these areas all over the planet, although many are unfamiliar to most people. Of note, these include the Bridgewater Triangle in Massachusetts, the Lake Michigan Triangle, the Nevada Triangle (which also includes parts of California), and the Dragon Triangle off the coast of Japan. All exhibit varying degrees of paranormal and supernatural activity, tragic accidents and disappearances, and sightings of extraterrestrials and strange creatures at much more heightened levels than most other areas of the world. While researchers have been chronicling the unusual phenomena in these areas for decades – sometimes centuries – the prevailing question has become, "What is the source of their power?"

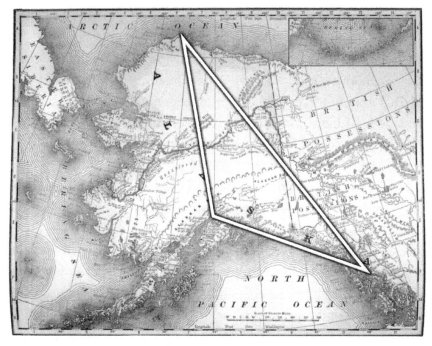

The approximate boundaries of the Alaska Triangle. These areas of the world are never "perfect" triangles. The areas' boundaries are vague, but three well-known points are chosen to define where most of the activity occurs.

The central figure of the Bridgewater Triangle area is the Hockomock Swamp, once known as "Devil's Swamp" to Colonial settlers. Here, witnesses have spotted vicious dogs with red eyes, a pterodactyl-like flying creature, Native American ghosts traversing the waterways in canoes, and glowing lights throughout the trees. Reports of Bigfoot activity also pocket the swamp, and there have been sightings of extraterrestrials in the area as well.

The possible source of the unusual activity in Lake Michigan, which includes lost ships, airplanes, and people vanishing into thin air, could be a ring of stones that was discovered under the lake in

2007. The stones rest under only 40 feet of water but seem to have a similar alignment to that of Stonehenge. Since ancient sites of power are known to tap into the Earth's energy grid, is this ring of stones from a lost civilization powering the lake to manifest this unusual activity?

In the Nevada Triangle, some believe the extensive number of plane crashes in the area are due to unusual wind conditions and a phenomenon referred to as a "Mountain Wave" which is an internal gravity wave within the mountain range that increases with elevation. Military plane crashes and disappearances in this area date as far back as 1943, with modern pilots still experiencing deadly problems in the area.

The Dragon Triangle near Japan in the Pacific, also known as The Devil's Sea, has legends extending as far back as 1000 BC in which Chinese fables spoke of dragons living under the water's surface who attacked passing sea vessels. An early historic account of trouble in the Dragon Triangle dates to the days of Kublai Khan, grandson of Genghis Khan, who lost some 40,000 crew aboard ships bound for an invasion of Japan in the late Thirteenth Century AD. Over the centuries, tale of ghosts on the sea permeated the local culture but the folklore seemingly became real and took on a life of its own just after World War II. In the 1940s and 50s, scores of Japanese fishing boats and military ships disappeared in the Dragon Triangle in the area between Miyake Island and Iwo Jima, so in 1952, the country sent an investigative team aboard *Kaio Maru No. 5* into the mysterious waters. Contact was lost, and long after they first set sail, scattered remnants of the ship were discovered floating in the sea. It's unknown what happened to the twenty-two crew members and nine scientists aboard. Following this incident, the Japanese government declared this area of the Dragon Triangle dangerous for marine voyage. What's the true nature of these "dragons" under the ocean that have caused so many tragedies for sea-faring vessels near Japan over the centuries?

Triangle areas of the world, such as the ones described above, contain vortices of energy which build up from the Earth's core and cause strange phenomenon to suddenly transpire, including unusual weather patterns, bizarre electromagnetic anomalies, and interdimensional portals. The most famous, of course, is the aforementioned Bermuda Triangle. Airplanes and ships travelling through these triangle areas report equipment failures and compasses running wild as well sightings of extraterrestrial crafts. Some disappear entirely, never to be heard from again. This energy is not constant, however. It ebbs and flows with the fluctuation of the Earth's geomagnetic field, so we don't consistently witness the strange phenomena that transpires in these areas, and we can't make it happen on demand. The Earth's core, along with the rest of the planet, is constantly in motion, bringing changes to magnetic fields all around the globe, greatly affecting some areas more than others.

> *Like all electric currents, these telluric currents travel better in some media than others. Ground with lots of metal or water within it conducts these natural, daily currents particularly well. Drier or less metallic ground conducts it less well. When these two types of land intersect we have what geologists call a conductivity discontinuity, and interesting things happen there. The ground current hitting this boundary has a tendency to either reinforce or weaken those daily magnetic fluctuations – sometimes by several hundred percent. This change in magnetic field strength in turn generates more electric current. So conductivity discontinuities are 'happening places'. Their magnetic fluctuations and ground currents are much higher than in surrounding areas. (Burke and Helberg. Seed of Knowledge, Stone of Plenty, Chapter 2)*

There are entire books written on the Earth's energy grid, telluric currents, and how ancient sites of power tap into these nodes of magnetic energy, and one I highly recommend is *The Divine Blueprint: Temples, Power Places and the Global Plan to Shape the Human Soul* by researcher Freddy Silva. To dive into all of that detail is beyond the scope of this book, but there are a handful of things we should note here before we examine this type activity occurring in Alaska.

A geographical survey of Alaska in 1965 by the United States Department of the Interior discovered as many as five different areas of distinct magnetic character in just the 100,000 square miles they surveyed (Alaska is 663,300 square miles large). In their interpretation of the magnetic data, the report stated:

> *"The magnetic profiles show numerous anomalies caused by variations in magnetization of the rocks, principally the mafic and ultramafic varieties, but also some granitic and metamorphic rocks. This magnetization is a combination of that induced by the present earth's field and the remanent magnetization – the latter tending to be largest in the mafic volcanic rocks. In some cases the direction of the remanent magnetization is reversed to give a negative anomaly. Several of these negative anomalies that cross basaltic dikes or serpentine bodies can be seen on profiles from the southern part of the area. Narrow step anomalies on the magnetic profiles are caused by rocks at or very near the surfaces, whereas some of the broader, smoother anomalies are probably caused by rocks at considerable depths."*

In other words, there are a significant number of different types of anomalies occurring in the region due to the geological structure of the Alaskan ground and the stone within it down to significant depths. These anomalies are also exacerbated by the Earth's magnetic influence, field, and currents upon these types of rocks and minerals within the area known as the Alaska Triangle. It's such a strange area that unusual weather patterns have been known to attract drifting sands from the Gobi Desert in China as high up as seven miles in the air and drop the particles on the Alaska Range in the heart of the Triangle.

Scientific studies in the Earth's magnetic field show us this field is volatile in nature, in both its strength and constantly shifting direction, and is connected to atmospheric phenomena and the planet's ecological system. For example, Professor Lisa Tauxe, head of the Paleomagnetic Laboratory at the Scripps Institution of Oceanography, during a study of the Earth's magnetic field on ancient artifacts in the Middle East stated, "Approximately 7,600 years ago, the strength of the magnetic field was even lower than today, but within approximately 600 years, it gained strength and again rose high to new levels."

A common point of confusion in this area of study has come in interchanging the term ley line with Earth energy lines. The telluric current, the actual magnetic energy of the Earth, are fields of magnetic current that run within the ground. Ley lines are terrestrial and connect specific points upon the landscape. In other words, the ley is simply the line we draw between the physical locations of these sites of power, whether those locations are temples, sets of standing stones, churches, pyramids, etc. They line up so succinctly because the ancients knew to build these sites upon hotspot nodes of the telluric current running through the earth, the telluric current being the actual natural electric current running beneath the Earth's surface.

Ley lines became recognized in the early Twentieth Century by Alfred Watkins in his 1925 book *The Old Straight Track*, but it took about 40 years before research by John Michell followed by the team of Hamish Miller and Paul Broadhurst brought the

*Ancient sites of power, such as pyramids, are known to have harnessed the
energy of the telluric currents within the Earth's energy grid. At the Step
Pyramid at Saqqara, Egypt, in June 2021.*

concept to the forefront. Traversing the English countryside, these
researchers rediscovered the alignment of ancient sites along
geodetic lines that became known as the Michael and Mary ley
lines due to the sheer number of temples, churches, and sanctuaries
along this axis dedicated to Michael the Archangel and St. Mary or
her mother, St. Anne. Extending this line outside of England, it
passes through Tiwanaku, the oldest temple site found in Bolivia,
and later through the mountain of Wuhzi, the holiest shrine of the
Chinese island of Hainan.

Ley lines such as the Michael and Mary tract, the Apollo-
Athena line through Europe, and many others are recognized all
over the world, connecting many historic sites of power. Finding a
ley line in Alaska is actually a difficult task since it's a rather
sparsely populated area of the world and you don't find ancient
temples and sites of power in the great white north. We're not
really interested in the leys, however. We're interested in what's
actually underneath and how that affects the surrounding area.

The term "ley line" has entered our lexicon as a catch-all
phrase for the telluric current phenomena, probably, because we

physically see ancient temples and sites of power with our own eyes rather than that mysterious current running through the ground. Plus, "ley line" is much easier and simpler to say than "telluric current." However, it's the telluric current in which we're most interested.

Experiments conducted by John Burke and Kaj Helberg and presented in their book *Seed of Knowledge, Stone of Plenty* showed that, "Electrodes planted at henge monuments in southern England revealed how their earthen ditches break the transmission of telluric ground current and conduct its electricity into the ditch, in effect concentrating the energy and releasing it at the entrance to the site, sometimes at double the rate of the surrounding land. This has led to the realization that stone circles, even mounds like Silbury Hill, behave like concentrators of electromagnetic energy." (Silva, Freddy. *The Divine Blueprint*, p. 181)

This is just one example, but we see this same phenomenon play out all over the world at locations such as Carnac, the Rollright Stones, Avebury, pyramids worldwide, and so many other ancient megalithic sites. This is why we use the term "ancient sites of power" – they're powered by the Earth's energy. This type of energy exists in Alaska as well, perhaps even more so, given the volatility of the land with its shifting tectonic plates and volcanic activity. We just don't see the accompanying human structures, unless they're buried under the ice somewhere, which is entirely possible.

When I filmed for the first season of *The Alaska Triangle* in May 2019, the producers asked me to scan along the face of Flattop Mountain outside of Anchorage with a set of dowsing rods and an electromagnetic field meter for unusual anomalies that may relate back to the activity of the vortex. It was kind of a shot-in-the-dark approach since we were only up on the mountainside for a day to shoot my interview segments, but it was a beautiful area in which to film. The camerawork of the crew was top-notch and the majestic view they captured of me traversing the mountain was breathtaking. I was thoroughly impressed with Wild Dream Entertainment in both their cinematography and their professionalism. While the EMF meter didn't yield much outside of small, negligible influxes, the dowsing rods were another matter.

As I stepped across the face of the mountain and held the rods outward, there was one particular spot in which the rod I held in my left hand turned inward toward the one I held in my right while the rod I held in my right hand remained transfixed straight outward. Walking out of the spot returned the rod in my left hand to its natural straight-forward position. To verify my findings, I did this several times, although the television show only shows me doing this once (they only have so much air time). The team was excited to have captured this interaction on film, but I wasn't yet done. My next test was to enter that hot spot again and then step up and down the face of the mountain to see if there was any change. While I did this, the rod in my left hand remained pushed inward toward the rod in my right hand while the rod in my right hand remained pointed straight ahead. Up and down the face of the mountain the rods remained fixed in this position, and I was able to draw a line from the top of Flattop Mountain pointed straight down toward Anchorage below us. Had I found a telluric current, one of those electromagnetic lines of the Earth's energy grid? Was this part of the vortex of the Alaska Triangle?

Other vernacular that seems to be commonly interchanged are the terms *vortex* and *portal*. We've already discussed, in brief, that a vortex is the swelling of the Earth's energy from the core of the planet, creating a myriad of unusual activity. So, what's a portal? A portal is a doorway into another dimension or some other place in time, perhaps even another location in the universe entirely. Portals are a potential result of the energy manifestation from vortices, some of that previously mentioned unusual activity

Flattop Mountain outside of Anchorage, Alaska.

created by them. So, yes, portals and vortices are certainly directly related to each other, but they are not the exact same thing.

When a vortex spawns a portal, it creates a link from our world to some other place in space-time. At this point, outside of an assortment of theories being tested in the lab, we don't have a means to control where a portal spawns and where it can potentially take us. If we had accomplished that then you would have already seen headlines about the creation of the world's first true time machine or the opening of a wormhole to another galaxy. The trick has always been in trying to figure out the catalyst. We're not sure what exactly kicks off these portals, but when they do appear, we could pass into another point in time, somewhere in the distant past or even the future, we could pass into an altered state of consciousness, or the portal could launch us to an entirely different realm. The ancients seemed to know much more about this type of energy control, and we're just starting the rediscover this knowledge today. We'll explore a few of these possibilities in our journey through this book.

One of the most interesting photos I've observed of supernatural phenomena was the capture of a portal opening at a cemetery in Earlsboro, Oklahoma. Unfortunately, I don't possess this photo, and I'm no longer in contact with the person who has it, so I can't present it here. However, I can tell you it appeared as if the middle of the image and onward toward the right had been torn open from our current existence, illuminated by waves of energy. The source of this energy was some sort of wavy electric-like rod in the middle of the photo, and from this rod stretched an opening toward the righthand side of the photograph. Through this tear that was created, one could see vague details of what appeared to be a sitting room beyond, something completely foreign to the cemetery. The original subject of this photograph was just a large bush that had far outgrown the headstone by which it was planted, nothing particularly special. Yet, in some alternate universe or time in history there sat access to someone's sitting room. Subsequent photos taken at that location have revealed nothing. So, what were the special conditions that caused the opening of the portal viewed in this one photograph? At this point, we honestly have no idea, but when we catch glimpses of this kind of supernatural phenomenon or unexplainable things suddenly occur in a location which has seen countless other examples of unexplainable activity, it heightens our curiosity and we go exploring for the truth, wherever it may take us.

Let's take this type of portal a step further and examine something called *interdimensional phasing*. This is another example outside the confines of Alaska, and it takes place in Harrisville, Rhode Island, at the home known as "The Conjuring House," the Eighteenth Century farmhouse upon which the first *Conjuring* movie was based, but the principles are relevant for the phenomena we'll examine in this book.

I had several interesting experiences at this house while specifically investigating the shadow phenomenon that occurs there during filming for *The Shadow Dimension* docu-series in September 2020. Most of the day was spent conducting interviews, but even during those low-key moments strange things occurred. I was in the upstairs bedroom that contains a chalkboard wall and was interviewing demonologist Keith Johnson about a bizarre experience he'd had with the exterior window in that room during his first visit to the house with his brother, Carl, in 1973. While I was questioning him, I suddenly began to feel extremely lightheaded and fought hard to prevent myself from rocking backward while I filmed. When Keith finished his story, I closed the camera and sat down on the bed near the interior window for a moment to collect myself. This window had been directly behind me, which is important to note for what happened later. Could this reaction have simply been from stress and fatigue? Perhaps. However, this was the room from which Carl had originally seen shadow smoke phenomenon billow up and move toward him during the 1973 investigation.

Later in the day, Carl and I were conducting an investigation of the middle room upstairs, and the entire room slowly started growing darker. It was extremely gradual, and as it darkened the air grew heavier. The moment we stated we were done, everything instantly lightened back up – the air, the light, everything.

What's even more interesting about this visit is a photograph I took while making a visual sweep of the house. In this photo, the area by the door and the interior window is quite hazy, almost like it's in motion, while the rest of the contents within the room are at a perfect standstill and clear. More intriguing is how the exterior window in the bedroom with the chalkboard, of which most is *not* visible *behind the wall*, is actually seen in almost its entirety within the room, transitioned to the right and covering a significant portion of the chalkboard. It appears as if some sort of interdimensional phasing was occurring when I captured the photo. Much of our discussion that day centered around Andrea Perron's assertion that the area is a portal cleverly disguised as a farmhouse. Had I captured a photograph of that portal's energy?

Is this energy from a portal around the window and doorway captured on camera? The exterior window in the other room is seen transitioned to the right.

While interviewing Andrea, whose family had lived in the house for 10 years and upon which the popular *Conjuring* film is based, we talked about those rooms, extensively. Before I even said anything to her about my experiences in that bedroom which had once been hers, she stated, "You know that [interior] window? I would very often see that very same smoke-like apparition form on the outside of the window beyond that wall in the center bedroom, and then it would seep down behind the window and go through the crack under the door and start to try to manifest in my room. I would say to it, 'You can't come in here right now. I don't know who you are. I'm doing my homework. You're not allowed in here right now. You need to go away.' I was always polite and respectful, but it always did. It would just shapeshift into a smoky haze and then just dissipate through the bottom crack of the door. But that meant it was going into the middle bedroom where I had two sisters that slept that night."

Was this interdimensional phasing and shadow activity caused by some sort of vortex energy present on the property? Given the vast amount of hauntings, strange activity, and UFO sightings at the property over the centuries, it certainly seems there must be some sort of energy like that there. One of the other experiences Andrea talks about occurring at the farmhouse is a *time slip* that happened directly below those rooms on the first floor. While helping her mother late one night, they suddenly witnessed an Eighteenth Century family appear in the dining room. The men sitting at a table that was not the Perron's turned and looked at Andrea's mother who was in the parlor, and made remarks that *she* was actually the ghost. We'll see these types of time slips play out in Alaska as well, but this is the type of strange phenomena that areas like this around the world can create.

Helping to power this phenomena at "The Conjuring House" is the construction of the well room in the basement (directly below these rooms). The room contains an open well filled with water, is constructed of limestone walls, and topping those limestone walls are slabs of granite whose primary mineral composition is quartz. This is like a perfect little power plant to help aid in generating the strange activity that occurs within the house.

In addition to energy from the Earth's core creating vortices, the sun also wreaks havoc in the polar regions of the world via the solar wind it blows out into space. Protons and electrons from the sun are regularly sent toward the Earth from solar flare activity in our star and have a greater chance of entering the atmosphere at the poles which are less protected, colliding with gas particles as they enter the atmosphere and creating the Aurora Borealis in the north and the Aurora Australis in the south. The altering of the upper atmosphere by this solar flare activity has been known to cause disruptions with electronic equipment and global positioning systems. The solar maximum, which is an enormous coronal mass ejection from the sun that occurs every eleven years, has the potential to knock out entire power grids on the ground. Given the thinner layer of protection in the polar regions and Alaska, the effect of such an ejection there would be far more substantial than elsewhere on the planet. Combining this energy with the telluric currents in the ground and the volatility in the area from earthquakes and volcanos, and you now have a situation that's ripe for strange and unusual – and potentially dangerous – things to occur.

The Earth's magnetic field protects us from much of the sun's activity that's launched our way, but solar flares still have an impact upon our planet.

How much more so could being in an area of the world such as this affect us when there's iron in our blood and magnetite in our brain that react to electromagnetic activity? When these solar flares penetrate our atmosphere and interact with our electronics, are they also interacting with us? Is this something we could harness to voluntarily enter into altered states of consciousness or to even open our own portals into other dimensions? We may not have mastered those possibilities yet (or remastered, most likely), but portal-creating potential is there, and it appears the phenomenon has occurred on its own, naturally. If we've lost knowledge from our ancient world, are these severely-impactful solar flares possibly an aspect of sun god worship that we haven't yet come to understand? Food for thought.

Also known as the Northern Lights, there appears to be some debate regarding the etymology of "Aurora Borealis," whether it originates from Latin or Greek. Whichever the case, ancient mythology from the Romans and Greeks essentially tells us the same thing – Aurora (or Eos) was the sister of Sol (Helios), the god and personification of the sun, and Luna (Selene), the goddess and personification of the moon. According to the tale, Aurora races across the early morning sky in her multi-colored chariot and creates the heavenly phenomenon to announce the approaching dawn of a new day to her siblings. While they may have not known specifically about protons and electrons, the ancients knew there was a relationship between the sun and atmospheric activity.

The sun's impact upon our planet is more significant than most other things in our universe. Without it, the Earth would just be a frozen rock floating around in space. We base our days off the sun, our seasons, our measurement of time. The sun's heat and its gravitational pull both significantly impact our weather patterns, and if, for some reason, the sun's rays are prevented from reaching the Earth properly, say by a meteor impact upon the planet creating a massive dust cloud … hello, ice age. So, if the influence of the sun is more impactful in Alaska because there is less protection there from solar flare activity, then it stands to reason that this is going to be a significant complementary component to the energy from the ground that's already impacting the area. It seems rather ironic that the sun should have such an influence in an area of the world that we typically associate with cold and not heat.

Volcanic activity has also had a dramatic effect on Alaska, and that includes a new discovery under the icy waters of the Aleutian Islands, the archipelago that stretches out from the mainland into the Bering Sea. Proposed by scientists near the end of 2020, six

Ash plume arising from Mount Cleveland on May 23, 2006, as seen from the International Space Station.

islands near the middle of the chain once thought to be separate volcanoes are now believed to be interconnected vents of a much larger volcano which slumbers underwater. The cluster of islands – Carlisle, Cleveland, Herbert, Kagamil, Tana, and Uliag – appear to be part of a caldera hidden by the ocean, which would explain why Mount Cleveland is one of the most active volcanoes in North America, according to John Power, a researcher with the U.S. Geological Survey at the Alaska Volcano Observatory. Calderas are formed when massive magma reservoirs in the Earth's crust explode, propelling far more ash and lava into the atmosphere than a standard stratovolcano, then collapse into the emptied magma chamber leaving behind its characteristic depression. For illustrative purposes, the oldest of Yellowstone National Park's three overlapping calderas in Wyoming smothered 5,790 square miles with ash when it erupted.

Alaska has also been home to the most powerful earthquake in U.S. history, the Great Alaskan Earthquake of 1964, the 9.2

Devastation in downtown Anchorage from the 1964 Great Alaskan Earthquake. It rocked the world on March 27 – Good Friday.

monster that devastated the region, killing 131, kicking off tsunamis that reached as far away as Japan and Hawaii, and ringing the Earth like a bell. It was so powerful that more than 1,200 miles away in Seattle the Space Needle swayed from the shock. The tsunamis took the most lives, obliterating towns along the Alaskan coast, but five also died when a tsunami hit Oregon and another twelve when one hit Crescent City, California. It was the second largest earthquake ever recorded in the world, next to Chile's 9.5 earthquake in 1960, rupturing 600 miles of the fault line and relieving approximately 500 years of stress buildup.

How much do these natural phenomena affect the area we've come to call the Alaska Triangle? That's what the rest of this book is about.

Chapter 2

MISSING AIRPLANES

Since 1988, over 16,000 people have gone missing in Alaska, which is an alarming number given the small population that resides there. The most notorious of these cases involve airplanes vanishing without a trace, never to be seen or heard from again. Of course, not every airplane that flies into the Alaska Triangle meets with some ill fate. Planes fly in and out of the Triangle all the time, as they do through the Bermuda Triangle in the Atlantic and elsewhere around the world, but the way these disappearances and strange phenomena occur in Alaska causes one to question if the vortex energy from the Triangle had an effect in these cases.

During my Air Force tour in April 1993, about a month prior to the 6.9 earthquake I experienced, a truly "only in Alaska" moment occurred when a Boeing 747 cargo jet taking off from the Anchorage airport suddenly lost its engine, and I seriously mean *lost*. The engine fell right off the airplane! Perhaps it was a serious defect, or perhaps, the forces of the triangle wreaked havoc upon the plane, but the engine tore right off the 747 and crashed into the parking lot of a local supermarket. Fortunately, the majority of the plummeting hulk landed on the backside of the lot where nobody had parked, but could you imagine walking out with your groceries and seeing a large metal object like an airplane engine plummet into the pavement? Debris and shrapnel rained down into the local neighborhoods, and people reported walking into their bedrooms to find shards of metal lodged into their floors with gaping holes in the ceiling above. Only in Alaska. Somehow, thankfully, there were zero injuries and the plane landed back at the airport safely.

Inspectors examine the damage on the Boeing 747 which lost its engine taking off from Anchorage in April 1993.

A spokesman for Boeing stated the airplane hit severe turbulence just after takeoff that day, causing the engine to shear away from the craft. What kind of turbulence causes something that large and weighing thousands of pounds to be ripped away from its vessel, plunging from an altitude of 1,800 feet?

This is just one of many strange accounts concerning aircraft in and around the Alaska Triangle.

Alaska's Mysterious Triangle

The Missing Douglas Skymaster

On January 26, 1950, two hours after a Douglas C-54D Skymaster airplane took off from Elmendorf Air Force Base, just next to Anchorage, headed for Great Falls Air Force Base in Montana, it disappeared without a trace. The weather called for mostly clear skies, only a few scattered clouds, and there was no reason to suspect anything was wrong with its final radio contact at 1:09 PM. However, at the very edge of the Alaska Triangle, near Snag in Yukon Territory, Canada, it disappeared. No wreckage or survivors have ever been found.

A massive joint U.S. and Canadian search commenced, covering over 350,000 square miles with 7,000 people involved and costing the equivalent of $10 million in today's dollars. Yet, with all of this effort nothing was ever found of the missing airplane nor of the 44 people who were on board. Oddly, a month later on March 1, a Canadian plane crashed near Snag in the same area in which the Douglas had gone missing. The Canadian plane was found relatively quickly and the crew only sustained light injuries. So, what happened to the C-54D Skymaster?

At the time the Douglas aircraft went missing, the United States and Canada had been scheduled to participate in a series of war games. These were canceled once the plane was reported missing, and many of the 20,000 troops who were to have participated in the games were deployed in search and rescue efforts for the missing aircraft. This became known as "Operation Mike." Personnel fanned out over the frosty terrain and a large aerial search commenced, including an area known as "the graveyard" of aircraft that had existed en route to Russia during World War II. Civilian reports from the surrounding communities were varied from park rangers, school children, and more, some claiming to have seen the aircraft and later hearing a thud while others claimed to have seen the aircraft then heard an explosion.

47

None of these alleged sightings were accurate. Reports of smoke clouds near Teslin, Yukon Territory, turned out to be vapor clouds from an ice fault, reported smoke signals near Waldo, British Columbia, turned out to be a logging camp, and one false report of a Douglas Skymaster sighting came from as far south as Edmonton, Alberta.

Four days into the search operation, a cryptic radio message was intercepted by a U.S. Air Force aircraft on its return trip from investigating a lead near Whitehorse, Yukon Territory, but it was difficult to discern the message and a return flight into the area revealed nothing. A couple days later, two more cryptic voice messages were intercepted in the Smith River area by a ground station, yet as quickly as the transmissions had started, they had stopped. Many believe these transmissions were broadcast from the crew of the missing Douglas airplane, but if so, why so few signals? And why were they so garbled and cryptic?

Severe winter weather moved into the area, suppressing the search efforts. Still, by the time the search was abandoned in the middle of February, the flight group had logged over 175 hours of air time scouring the hard landscape for an airplane that would never be seen again. The rescue efforts were certainly thorough.

Several theories as to what happened to the missing Douglas on January 26, 1950, abound. Some people believe the Douglas aircraft disappeared as a result of UFO activity. Alaska is a prime location for UFO sightings, as we'll seen in Chapter 6, and several were reported just before and just after the Douglas aircraft went missing, including one near Kodiak just three days prior to the disappearance and another just two days after at Elmendorf Air Force Base. We'll cover UFO activity in Alaska in later chapters, but there are many people that believe extraterrestrial activity is heightened in Alaska and the missing Douglas could have fallen victim to ETs.

A Douglas C54-D Skymaster in flight.

Some believe the high electromagnetic activity in the Alaska Triangle area opened a portal into another dimension through which the plane passed through. The strange, sporadic radio transmissions are believed to be emanating from this other dimension. While this may seem far-fetched to some, it's not as crazy as it sounds. Later in this book, we'll explore the possibilities of sound waves traversing through other dimensions and, possibly, time.

If the Douglas Skymaster did pass through a portal, where did it actually go? Did it disappear into another universe, another star system, perhaps? Or was it simply transported to the exact same location but at another point in time? If it did move in time, how would the peoples in that location have viewed this large, loud aircraft barreling through the sky? Could they, perhaps, have thought it to be a thunderbird? We'll dive more into that topic when we explore cryptid encounters in Chapter 7, but these are all possibilities.

A National Incident

The unfortunate event that really gave the Alaska Triangle its notoriety was the disappearance of a plane on October 16, 1972, carrying the United States House Majority Leader Hale Boggs, Alaska Congressman Nick Begich, aide Russell Brown, and pilot Don Jonz. The largest search and rescue mission in U.S. history to that point was launched, much larger than what was ever put together for the missing Douglas Skymaster, spanning an area of 325,000 square miles and more than 3,600 hours of search time. Even an SR-71 spy plane was pressed into service for the search. To this day, nothing has ever been found.

Boarding a Cessna 310C, the four set out from Anchorage International Airport at 9:00 AM with a course set for Juneau. The flight plan set by Jonz wasn't any different than the thousands of flights plans set before with a destination of Juneau, and Jonz, an expert pilot, had flown this route countless times beforehand. However, just before reaching Portage Pass, the airplane completely disappeared. The radio call from the Cessna to Flight Service 10 minutes after take-off to file the flight plan was the last anyone ever heard from them. As is so typical for the mysteries of the Alaska Triangle, the recording of that transmission was lost. When the plane failed to show up in Juneau and with lack of any further radio contact, the search was immediately launched and given top priority considering who was on board.

Hale Boggs had dissented against the Warren Commission, the investigation into the John F. Kennedy assassination which ruled the death was caused by a single bullet. He had plenty of political enemies throughout the country, and there are several conspiracy theories that suggest a bomb was on board the Cessna to eliminate Boggs. Some believe that it wasn't his dissention against the Warren Commission that may have gotten him assassinated but it was his Croatian heritage and his Croatian nationalism that may have made him a target for Serbians during a time in which tensions were running high in the former Yugoslavia[1].

Of course, the disappearance may have had nothing to do with an assassination attempt and may have simply been navigational problems through the Portage Pass. The pass is only about a mile wide and the mountains on either side rise sharply to 4,000 feet creating a "geographic vortex generator" for nearly six miles. These types of vortices are aerodynamic elements that stimulate macro-vortical motions and provide momentum enhancement in the vicinity of a wall. That sounds like a mouthful, but basically this type of airflow has an affect on craft trying to fly through it,

---

[1] There were three different iterations of Yugoslavia, the last ending in 2003. The Boggs – Begich disappearance happened during the second iteration which ended in 1992, but the roots to its demise are believed to have started in the 1970s. https://www.jstor.org/stable/2620829

especially as it nears its boundaries, in this case, tall mountains. The type of vortex generator at the Portage Pass, however, is one in which during low weather conditions, as was the case that October morning, can actually help planes slip through the pass unscathed. But was it enough to deal with the deteriorating conditions that day which called for icing, poor visibility, and turbulence? Or did the Alaska Triangle amp up the vortex generator to new levels that made passage even more treacherous? Or in another scenario, could a portal have been generated as has been speculated regarding the missing Douglas Skymaster back in 1950?

Although an extensive search was conducted twice over throughout the Portage Pass, no wreckage or evidence of the airplane's presence or of its passengers was ever discovered. Some say the Cessna must have made it through or it would have otherwise been located. But if it did make it through then where did it go? Decades later, it's still a mystery.

The Alaska Triangle's Broken Arrow

What may be even scarier and more concerning than a complete disappearance of an airplane is the time a nuclear bomb was lost in the Alaska Triangle – a bomb that is still a "broken arrow" to this day. In another tragic event in 1950, a B-36 bomber taking off from Eielson Air Force Base near Fairbanks, Alaska, had to jettison its Mark IV nuclear bomb (comparable to the payload that was dropped on Nagasaki) over the Pacific Ocean when the plane began to malfunction.

The date was February 13, not even three weeks after the Douglas Skymaster had gone missing near Snag when the B-36 and its crew of 17 took off on a 5,500-mile training mission which included Montana, its "target" of San Francisco, and finally landing at Carswell Air Force Base in Texas. The intention of the test run was to simulate a bombing run on the Soviet Union. Although an atomic warhead was on board the plane and contained large amounts of uranium, authorities insist that it did not have its plutonium core nor could it trigger a nuclear blast. Feel free to debate.

B-36 bomber from the same bombardment wing as the plane that crashed.

While in flight heading south over the Pacific, the plane began to ice up and three of the engines had to be shut down when they caught fire. With the weight of the bomb expediting the plane's descent, the decision was made to jettison the warhead into the ocean. This was essential protocol for Captain Harold Barry and his crew in order to keep the weapon out of the hands of the enemy. Eyes widened onboard when the "salvo" button was hit and nothing happened. Strange malfunction? Upon hitting the button a second time, the bomb bay doors opened and the Mark IV dropped, detonating its conventional explosives on the way down, its remains falling into the ocean.

For the crew, however, they needed to parachute off the B-36 or go down with it. Setting the plane on autopilot out toward the open Pacific Ocean, the 17-member crew jumped to assumed safety, but not all would be recovered. Five of the crewmembers were never found, including weaponeer, Theodore Schreier. Schreier was a former airline pilot and had enough skill to attempt to continue flying the plane as the rumors began circulating at that time. These stories suggested that Captain Barry had seen the B-36 turn sharply after he jumped, and in fact, the plane did not end up out at sea as he had set the autopilot. The B-36 flew in the opposite direction and eventually crashed into Mount Kologet in British Columbia, the wreckage lost for three years. The crew ended up scattered in the darkness of Princess Royal Island. Schreier was never found on Princess Royal Island, nor in the wreckage of the plane on Mount Kologet, so the rumors that he may have stayed aboard to try to pilot the plane can't be substantiated, but where he or the other four missing crew members ended up no one knows for certain.

There are several areas here in which the effects of the Alaska Triangle may have played a part – the malfunctioning of the plane upon icing, the salvo button not working immediately, the autopilot turning the B-36 in the opposite direction, and five of the crew members disappearing without a trace. It seems this period of time in 1950 was a window rife with unusual activity between disappearing airplanes, UFO sightings, and a bomber crash resulting in a broken arrow.

Other Airplane Tragedies

While tragedies like those described above garner most of the press regarding tragedies in the Alaskan air, there have been scores of flights over the decades that have gone completely missing in the Alaska Triangle.

On May 3, 1992, a Cessna 340 carrying three brothers – Kent,

Scott, and Jeff Roth – along with their two friends, Brian Barber and Tim Thornton, took off from Yakutat after a fishing expedition heading back to Anchorage and was never seen again. The last report in from Kent, the pilot, to air traffic control was that the plane was at about 12,000 feet. Jeff's wife, Gayle, listened to the FAA tapes of the transmissions that day and thought she heard several minutes after the last official transmission something about "6,000 feet" and "icing conditions," but an enhancement of the tapes by the FBI revealed nothing.

Two decades later on September 9, 2013, Alan Foster also disappeared flying out of Yakutat. Foster had purchased a Piper PA-32 Cherokee in Atlanta, Georgia, and was flying the plane over 4,000 miles home to Anchorage. He was on the last leg of his journey, only 360 miles from home when he stopped in Yakutat to refuel. About 42 miles after take-off, Foster's plane dropped off the radar and was never seen again. During the search and rescue efforts, a small electronic ping was heard from the area of Mount Eberly in the Wrangell-St. Elias National Park and Preserve, pinged a second time, and was never heard again. It's unknown if this ping was at all Foster or his plane.

It's not out of the question that some of these aircraft won't ever be found. In August 1958, Clarence Rhode, the Alaska regional director of the U.S. Fish and Wildlife Service at that time, along with this son and another Fish and Wildlife agent went missing in the Arctic National Wildlife Refuge when they took flight for a cache of supplies at Porcupine Lake. They weren't seen again until 1979 when two hikers found the wreckage of their Grumman Goose near the head of the Ivishak River. It appeared the plane collided with the mountainside at 5,700 feet and became hidden by the vegetation below.

Similarly, Colony Glacier finally gave up its secret in 2012 of a C-124 Globemaster and its 52 men that had gone missing in 1952 while en route to Elmendorf Air Force Base. The aircraft's tail section emerged from the glacier at the 8,100-foot level near the top of Mount Gannet, having moved 12 miles with the ice over the span of 60 years.

For others, however, the Alaska Triangle holds tight to their mysteries and refuses to divulge any clues to their whereabouts, even in this modern age of high technology.

2003: A pilot and two passengers in a Cessna 180 was lost flying from Hallo Bay to Homer.

2004: A glacier tour flight with four passengers disappeared after taking off from Sitka.

2009: A Beechcraft Bonanza with a husband and wife on their way to Whitehorse from Wolf Lake completely vanished.

These are just a handful of tragic tales, but there are so many more for which anguished families seek answers.

Chapter 3

LOST AT SEA

Like its sister triangle in the Atlantic's Bermuda region, the Alaska Triangle is also known for its strange and unusual – and sometimes tragic – activity surrounding boats, ships, and sea-faring vessels. Traveling the waters of the Earth has always been a dangerous proposition, and scores of mariners from all parts of the world over the millennia have recounted a colorful array of strange tales from their nautical adventures. Alaska is no different, and in many ways is probably more even more dangerous given its treacherous waters.

Summertime on the seas of Alaska is generally mild, but as the fall and winter seasons settle in, that's when the Triangle bears its brutal teeth. Winds off the Pacific blast islands and seaboard towns, and gusts have been known to roll and capsize poorly loaded ships. Fog can hang so thick and low that shoals and reefs go unseen until a vessel runs aground, arctic winds will coat ships in ice in a matter of minutes, and storms will kick up so quickly and heavily dumping enormous amounts of snow onto ship decks. All of that is before we even consider the strange electromagnetic properties of the region that may affect instrumentation and account for many of these tragedies. Countless numbers of ships and people have been lost in the perilous, frigid Alaskan waters.

SS Princess Sophia – The Alaskan Titanic

On October 24, 1918, the passenger liner *SS Princess Sophia* ran aground on Alaska's Vanderbilt Reef, and a day later it and at least 353 people aboard the ship disappeared into the icy waters. The lone survivor, sadly, was a single English Setter dog covered in oil. Since that tragic autumn day wrought with high winds and torrential snow, this heartbreaking maritime accident has become known as "The Alaskan *Titanic.*"

The *Sophia* was considered a newer ship in 1918; its maiden voyage set sail just six years prior on June 7, 1912, and it pretty much kept the same course throughout that time from Skagway to Vancouver, although she did spend a short amount of time serving as a troop carrier during World War I. According to *The Sinking of the Princess Sophia* by Ken Coates and Bill Morrison:

> *A man who sailed on the* Princess Sophia *in the summer of 1915 remembers her as a 'strong ship'; she had a large mast and boom on the forward deck capable of lifting heavy loads into the freight hold. ... She was not a particularly fast vessel – top speed was between 12 and 13 knots – but she was sturdy and comfortable, and handled well in all weather.*

The *Princess Sophia* left Skagway, Alaska, that fateful October day en route to Juneau more than three hours behind schedule. Skagway had become overcrowded with travelers trying to make their way south before the harsh winter set in, and at least 600 to 700 people were queued up waiting to depart when the *Sophia* had

The SS Princess Sophia *in 1912.*

docked just days beforehand. The ship had just returned from a voyage carrying 268 souls southward and would be packing in as many as she could for another run on October 23, hopefully escaping the encroaching frigidity. Back in Vancouver, the *Princess Sophia* had just been fitted with new buoyancy tanks in case of emergency, part of the changing regulations after fallout from the *Titanic* disaster, so she was able to increase her passenger capacity by 100 and take more people onto the ship. Unfortunately, in this case, that spelled doom for 100 more passengers than the *Sophia* would have usually carried.

Captain Leonard Locke, a workman-like and strict captain by most accounts, quickly navigated the Lynn Canal following the ship's departure from Skagway. Locke may have had a bit of a romantic streak within him – he once wrote a poem for a young female passenger who remarked that no one had said goodbye to her[2] – but he was generally considered a disciplinarian and

---

[2] 'The good ship sails, I go to sea; but no one says good-bye to me' by Captain Leonard Locke, preserved by J.L. McPherson of the Seattle Chamber of Commerce to whom Locke gave a copy.

believed in an honest day's wage for an honest day's work. So, the fact the *Princess Sophia* would have veered so far off course under his guidance along a route he had sailed many times is rather mind-boggling. Yet it did by over a mile within the confines of a channel only six and a half miles wide. Was the strict disciplinarian suddenly out of character and reckless, pressed to make up for lost time after the late departure, or had the electromagnetism of the Alaska Triangle affected the ship's instrumentation, directing the vessel astray?

The weather may have also wreaked havoc with the ship's guidance as conditions quickly deteriorated into a mounting snow storm. The wind kicked up out of the north at about 50 miles per hours as the *Sophia* passed Battery Point at 11:00 PM, just 16 miles out from Skagway, and snow started pounding the ship. However, Captain Locke had seen worse storms in his career, and the crew was confident of his abilities and decision-making. W.C. Dibble, a fireman aboard the *Sophia*, once wrote to his wife:

> *One lady passenger of our boat said to our Captain the other night, 'Captain, do you know where every rock is?' and the Captain replied he was not sure about that, but knew where deep water was and keeps in it if possible, and everybody says that Captain Locke knows every inch up to Skagway, so we are safe as far as that goes.*

Where the Vanderbilt Reef lies, however, the main channel of the Lynn Canal narrows to two and a half miles, leaving less room for error in navigation than the rest of the canal. Captain Locke, the seasoned veteran, was aware of this, of course, yet at 2:00 AM on the morning of October 24 the *Princess Sophia* was cruising right down the middle of the Lynn Canal when the deeper waters were on the east side. Had there been a miscalculation by Captain Locke or the pilot, Jerry Shaw? Had the howling winds or the volatile tides altered the way the ship approached this part of the canal? There's never been a clear answer as to what exactly happened that night, the course of events shrouded in mystery murkier than the stormy waters, but we do know that at 2:10 AM the *Princess Sophia* crashed into the Vanderbilt Reef.

This wasn't a full-frontal kind of crash. The passenger liner ground up onto the reef, scraping and clawing its way across the rock at a dozen knots, jagged stone tearing at its steel hull. The crew were thrown across the deck like rag dolls while sleeping passengers were tossed out of their beds. Goods and supplies all throughout the ship thrashed about before the vessel finally ground to a halt, trapped. Then an eerie silence settled across the *Princess Sophia*, save but for the droning song of the howling wind.

In documentation rescued from the wreckage of the ship, passenger John Maskell, on his way back to England to be married, described the situation to his fiancée in a letter:

> *We struck a rock last night which threw many from their berths, some were crying, some too weak to move, but the lifeboats were swung out in all readiness, but owing to the storm would be madness to launch.*

That became the desperate plight of the *Princess Sophia* – trapped on a reef in a storm which made it too dangerous for anyone to save them. Distress calls went out and a rescue flotilla out of Juneau was assembled, but the rescue vessels soon ran into the same issue the *Sophia* had – the weather. Most also weren't equipped well enough to house the number of voyagers the passenger liner had been carrying. But that shortcoming wouldn't matter.

The wind and waves forced the *Princess Sophia* further up onto the reef. It was a precarious situation for any attempted rescue operation. At low tide the ship was surrounded by rocks and at high tide the swells were so powerful that if any lifeboats attempted an approach they would smash against the rocks as the waves surged up and down. James Davis, master of the *Estebeth*, described what he saw of the *Sophia* through the storm:

> *She had a big rent in the bow, fore and aft, and the water was pouring out of her in a big rush – running out say probably two or three hundred gallons a minute – something like that – probably a four or six inch seam. Her propeller wasn't two feet off her natural water line.*

That was another precarious problem for the *Princess Sophia* – it didn't appear she wasn't going to get back into the water. At low tide she was completely surrounded by rock, and at high tide, while most of the rock was covered, it wasn't even enough to float in a lifeboat without it meeting some perilous end.

As more ships braved the storm and joined the rescue flotilla, Captain Locke setup successful wireless communications with Captain J.W. Leadbetter of the *USS Cedar*. It's a controversial point in the tragedy, but Leadbetter defended Locke who was criticized for warning off rescue boats until better weather conditions arrived. Captain Locke seemed optimistic that the *Princess Sophia* was firmly entrenched on Vanderbilt Reef and wasn't going anywhere anytime soon, stating his crew, "had examined the rock and they were resting securely in a cradle on the reef, the vessel was in no danger whatever." Davis from the *Estebeth* went as far as trying to lower a skiff into the water to attempt a rescue, but once he got a better look at the waves crashing against the rocks, he abandoned what would have been a doomed mission.

Leadbetter stated he still never observed conditions that would have allowed the evacuation of the *Princess Sophia* the following day on October 25. Passengers aboard the ship were tired and

The Princess Sophia *trapped on the Vanderbilt Reef. October 24, 1918.*

weary, water had filled the front compartment, and the main steam pipe had broken, temporarily knocking out the power. The hours dragged on as rescue ships continued to approach in vain attempts at figuring out some sort of solution to the mounting problem. The already vicious wind was actually gaining speed as the snow and spray continued to pound the ship. Captain Leadbetter made a couple tries at anchoring the *Cedar* about 500 yards from the *Sophia* hoping to run a line and ferry passengers over, but the merciless wind thwarted all attempts. Some estimates put the gusts as much as 100 miles per hour. All anyone could do was wait for the weather to break. The ragtag, weathered and weary passengers and crew of the *Princess Sophia* settled in for another long, frigid night while the rescue flotilla left to refresh, refuel, and figure out how to approach evacuating the *Sophia* the following morning.

Having retreated to Sentinel Island, Captain Leadbetter of the *Cedar* and Captain J.J. Miller of the *King and Winge* formulated a plan, although any plan required some sort of break in the weather. When they'd just finished their meeting and Miller was returning to his ship at about 4:50 PM, the wireless on the *Cedar* squawked. The message was from David Robinson, the wireless operator aboard the *Princess Sophia*: "Ship foundering on reef. Come at once."

Captain Leadbetter immediately began preparing to steam his ship back to Vanderbilt Reef while also wiring the oil tanker *Atlas* and calling out to Captain Miller and the *King and Winge* as the *Cedar* set off. At 5:20 PM the wireless squawked again with Robinson desperately pleading from the *Sophia*, "For God's sake hurry! The water is coming in my room!" There was more that followed, but it was indiscernible.

The wireless operator aboard the *Cedar* told Robinson to conserve his waning battery power and to only use it when necessary. Robinson anxiously responded, "All right, I will. You talk to me so I know you're coming." That was the last anyone heard from the *SS Princess Sophia*.

Captain Leadbetter and the *Cedar* battled the storm as they pushed northward toward Vanderbilt Reef in a complete whiteout. The snow was so thick and the wind so fierce that when they passed within 500 yards of the Sentinel Island lighthouse they could not hear the foghorn nor see the light. The farther they went the worse the weather got. Finally, fearing for the safety of his own ship and crew, Leadbetter had to return to the anchorage at Sentinel Island. Even while trying to return to safety, the storm was so terrible the *Cedar* came within 20 feet of crashing into the *King and Winge*.

With no other recourse, the rescue ships were stranded until morning to discover what may have happened to the *Princess Sophia*. On that morning of October 26, the snow was still falling heavily, but the weather had let up enough to trek up to Vanderbilt Reef. The *Cedar* was first on the scene in which the reef had been stripped of its quarry, completely bare, and only the top twenty feet of the *Sophia*'s foremast protruded out of the waters nearby.

Captain Leadbetter messaged the *Atlas* with news of the tragedy:

We made out the Sophia which has slid off and only mast showing. Rough sea breaking over reef, and gale and thick snow. Unable to get close so far. Looks like she must have broken in the middle as there is only one mast showing.

It's hard to know exactly what happened that fateful night, but it appeared that after forty hours of being locked into place on the Vanderbilt Reef, the wind and waves finally began winning their battle against the *Princess Sophia* and started to lift the stern off the reef. Once this action began, the wind was able to spin the passenger liner a full 180 degrees and started ripping it off the rock and into the sea. As it did so, the hull was gashed open to the point that nearly the entire bottom of the ship was gone by the time it entered the water. Oil rushed out, icy water rushed in, and the boilers exploded.

There was a mad dash to the lifeboats, but it was really too late. Most people didn't make it – many were actually still caught unawares in their staterooms – and those few that did manage to launch a lifeboat met the fate that Captain Locke, Captain Leadbetter, and all the rest feared. They were caught in a swell that crashed their lifeboats into the reef. Those that jumped from the ship into the frigid waters not only suffered from hypothermia within minutes but were also suffocated and weighed down by the massive amount of oil that had spilled out everywhere. Most watches on the victims had stopped at about 5:50 PM that evening, about the time Captain Leadbetter and the *Cedar* pushing northward were halted in their tracks by the storm and were forced to turn around. Even if Leadbetter had decided to keep pressing onward he would have been too late.

The rescue mission suddenly turned into a tragic search for the bodies of the victims. Fighting the brutish weather and fearing bodies could be washed out to open sea, the rescue teams worked as quickly as they could to find and lift victims out of the water. The weather had washed away much of the debris from the location of the sunken *Sophia*, and found all throughout the channel were large patches of oil littered with wreckage and bodies, some clumping along the shorelines.

When news of the *Princess Sophia*'s demise reached Juneau, the town was shocked at the horror but began preparations for the sudden intake of hundreds of human remains. What they received when the weather finally began to break and bodies could be recovered was truly a gruesome sight. Of the first 162 bodies recovered, only two had drowned; the rest had died of suffocation from the massive oil spill. Oil had caked over these victims making it difficult to tell they were actually human beings, and they had to be thoroughly cleaned. Volunteer residents of Juneau worked around the clock during the recovery where local businesses were turned into makeshift morgues. These local businesses are still haunted to this day, reporting screams and icy breaths throughout their establishments, and at times the sightings of apparitions of the passengers of the *Princess Sophia* have been reported at these locations as well.

To this day, the reverberations of the tragedy are still felt throughout the entire region, and what truly happened to the *Princess Sophia* – how it got caught on the Vanderbilt Reef and how it sank – remain much of a mystery.

Eldred Rock Light and the Clara Nevada Mystery

We're getting a bit ahead of ourselves with the tragedy of the *Princess Sophia* since 20 years prior there had been another notorious tragedy in the *Clara Nevada*, one which may also be a murder mystery. Located within that same Lynn Canal is the fabled Eldred Rock Light (officially listed in the National Register of Historic Places as Eldred Rock Lighthouse) which was built very early in the Twentieth Century following a number of notorious shipwrecks, including the *Clara Nevada* which ran aground – or exploded – on Eldred Rock in 1898. The mystery of the *Clara Nevada* and what exactly happened to the ship is famous for its legend of lost gold which has yet to be found as of the time of this writing.

In February 1898, witnesses in Seward City (now Comet), Alaska, reported suddenly seeing an orange fireball upon the waters within the Lynn Canal in the direction of where the tramp steamer the *Clara Nevada* had last been seen heading straight into a terrible storm. Steeped in legend, the *Clara Nevada* is said to have been carrying a load of gold from the Klondike, and some tales suggest the steamer could have been pillaged by pirates, the explosion the result of a robbery gone bad. It took eleven years for the hull of the ship to be found, and the only body ever discovered was that of the purser. The entire event is shrouded in mystery worthy of the Alaska Triangle.

The Klondike gold rush in the late 1890s, while it occurred in Canada, had a significant impact in Alaska as thousands of people scrambled to the port of Seattle for boats bound for the northerly U.S. territory where they disembarked and trekked to the Klondike area hoping to strike it rich. Ships which had been moldering wrecks were pressed back into action in significant disrepair and grossly overloaded. For example, a ship known as the *Islander* which made the journey was reportedly 100 tons overloaded with a human capacity that was about 150 too many and also included 600 dogs, 8 oxen, and 50 to 75 horses. The gold rush was big money for anyone who could manage ferrying people and supplies up the coast, and regulations were nowhere near as stringent at they are today. This was pre-*Titanic*, after all. If you could squeeze it on the ship and make a profit, it was loaded onboard.

The *Clara Nevada* was originally named the *Hassler* and

The Clara Nevada *during her maiden voyage in 1898.*

served as a survey vessel for the United States Coast and Geodetic Survey from 1872 until 1897 when, after a quarter century of service, she was deemed not seaworthy enough to continue her mission. She was sold to the Pacific & Alaska Transportation company, one of the many newly-formed organizations looking to cash in on the shipping demand to the Klondike, and was renamed the *Clara Nevada* after a popular actress at the time. She was a steamer at a length of 154 feet and could carry a crew and passengers up to 200 along with 300 pounds of cargo.

The *Clara Nevada* flirted with danger all throughout her "maiden" voyage[3]. She collided with the U.S. Revenue cutter *Grant* while backing out of her berth in Seattle, she crashed into the dock and damaged her bowsprit when she landed at Port Townsend, and she battled a hellish storm sailing northward, arriving too late at Juneau to unload the dynamite she carried. The journey of the steamer was such a calamity that the passengers threatened to mutiny, holding a meeting on deck and writing out a

---

[3] Although the steamer had been in service for 25 years as the *Hassler*, since she had been renamed, the 1898 journey for the *Clara Nevada* was considered her maiden voyage.

petition in a failed attempt to abandon ship in Port Townsend. According to north-bound passenger Charles Jones of Dalles, Oregon:

I was afraid the Clara Nevada *would be wrecked from the time she left Seattle until Skagway was reached. We smashed into the revenue cutter* Grant *when we were backing out of Yesler's Dock; we rammed into almost every wharf at which we tried to land; we blew out three* [boiler] *flues; we floundered around in rough waters until all the passengers were scared almost to death; we witnessed intoxication among the officers and heard them cursing each other until it was sickening.*

The steamer's chaotic arrival at Skagway was as grand as the one she made at Port Townsend, crashing into the pier and shattering three or four of the piles. It took about two hours for the confused ship to dock. The *Clara Nevada* offloaded its cargo and weary passengers then embarked on the trek back south into a storm never to be seen again.

On the evening of February 5, 1898, witnesses in Seward City (now Comet), Alaska, reported seeing a sudden orange fireball upon the waters within the Lynn Canal about eight miles from the *Clara Nevada*'s final resting place, and stated, "embers were seen to fly into the sky at great height," according to a *Seattle Times* article that February 23.

The storm grew fierce, preventing anyone from immediately venturing out into the night to inspect what had happened. By the time the *Rustler* headed out the investigate, nothing was left of the old steamer that had left Skagway. Debris began washing up on shore, including clothing, photographs, and furniture. A hatch cover with the name *Hassler* also washed up, creating some initial confusion over which ship had actually gone down.

Aboard the *Rustler* searching for possible survivors, United States Customs Inspector T.A. Marquam spotted the bulk of the wreck near the north shore of Eldred Rock, stating the, "hull was lying in about four fathoms [24 feet] of water, and her outline could be seen distinctly." To get a positive identification of the vessel, Marqaum sent a diver into the waters who observed, "a great black hole where the boiler room had been."

Marquam continued his search for survivors but found none at that time. Exacerbating the search was the fact that 18 inches of snow had been dumped on the area by the storm, so even finding a body washed up on shore proved impossible. In fact, only one body associated with the *Clara Nevada* wreck has ever been discovered, and a March 1898 dive at Eldred Rock to specifically recover bodies resulted in none being found. Precisely how many perished is unknown since the passenger list was lost with the ship, but from his research, historian Steven C. Levi states in book *The Clara Nevada* that, "combining the list of the dead from all newspaper articles, there were at least forty-six individuals aboard identifiable by name and one corpse[4]. But several newspapers stated a handful of women were onboard, for whom no names were given, as well as seven Klondikers, again with no names. There is also evidence to support the contention that there were at least three stowaways on board. Probably, the best count would be in the neighborhood of fifty-seven."

The tragedy garnered plenty of spotlight, but the *Clara Nevada* suddenly became legendary when rumors began circulating that $165,000 in gold had been aboard the ship when it went down. Adjusting for inflation, $165,000 in 2021 dollars is $5.4 million[5]. Thus began the great mystery of a ghost treasure ship that went down in the Alaska Triangle. The biggest question on everyone's

---

[4] The deceased body of a William Malloy was being transported south aboard the *Clara Nevada*.

[5] According to officialdata.org's inflation calculator.

mind is what happened to the gold?

First of all, there was great debate as to what actually took down the *Clara Nevada*. While the diver Marquam sent into the water to view the wreck stated there was a, "great black hole where the boiler had been," a blackened hull is more commiserate with a dynamite blast rather than a boiler explosion. What's more, a boiler explosion would have quickly extinguished any fire, but witnesses reported seeing an orange fireball and embers reaching, "into the sky at great height." At this point, we'll assume the orange fireball was fire-related and not an early UFO sighting, although in the Alaska Triangle you can never be 100% certain. After the discovery of a fire hose was found, "attached to the hydrants and coupled to the pumps," within the wreckage, the official conclusion reached by the Steamboat Inspection Service in August 1898 was that a fire had broken out on the ship, "and during the frantic fight to keep the flames from the place where there was stored powder and dynamite the officers lost their bearings and, incidentally, control of the ship." Eighteen years later, Alaskan hard-hat diver C.F. Stagger stirred up more controversy on the matter after spending two days at the wreck farming kelp and salvaging copper and brass by stating he was, "positive from the examination made that the vessel had not caught on fire as was generally supposed and that the wreck was caused by something else, most likely a submerged rock." Pun intended, the waters are certainly muddied on how the ship sank.

There are no official survivors of the tragedy, but a discovery in April 1898 fanned the flames of the *Clara Nevada* legend. Newspapers reported that a steamer named *Seaolin* had spotted a small boat on the beach near Seward City (Comet) that contained a roll of blankets and a life preserver from the *Clara Nevada*. A second blanket roll was discovered nearby next to the remains of a campfire and a life preserver that had been singed, perhaps by a fire on the doomed steamer. Opening the roll of blankets revealed clothing belonging to a "Geo. Kasey" and papers concerning purchases of goods made by William Hemming of Rockport, Indiana, as well as a memorandum signed, "Logsdon." Modern historian Steven C. Levi tracked down these individuals and discovered through Hemmings' granddaughter (the last name as reported in the papers neglected the 's' at the end) and she revealed that both her grandfather and his friend, Kasey, had indeed ventured off to Alaska in 1897 and returned a few years later. Kasey's name appears in the 1900 Alaska census record as a laborer for the Juellin Gold Mine near Berners Bay which is just a few miles from Comet (Seward City) and only 10 nautical miles from Eldred Rock where the wreck of the *Clara Nevada* rests. The two men were almost certainly survivors of the *Clara Nevada*, and Alaskan historian Bob De Armond goes as far as to suggest that they may have actually been stowaways, hiding in a lifeboat and skirting away to safety when whatever happened aboard the *Clara Nevada* began.

Steven C. Levi also spent significant time tracking down another potential survivor of the tragedy, Captain Charles H. Lewis – and found him. Within months of the *Clara Nevada* going down Lewis was operating the *William H. Evan*s, another steamer, along the Alaska coastline. The Captain had nearly as bad luck with the *Evans*, eventually ending up stuck on a sand bar trying to traverse the Yukon River. The ship remained trapped there for nearly three years. Lewis finished his career working for the Baltimore and Carolina Steamship Company and died in Baltimore on June 7, 1917. How he escaped the *Clara Nevada* is still a mystery.

Did any of these survivors make off with the gold? Was there a conspiracy to rob the ship of its riches and slip silently away into the frigid night? Was there even a possible murder aboard the *Clara Nevada*? Of all the souls lost during this tragedy, there was only one body ever found – George Foster Beck, the purser – and even his discovery was shrouded in mystery as three different newspapers gave very different stories as to how and where his body was found. Was Beck murdered to gain access to the gold or was he a person involved in the plot to steal the gold and perished during the robbery, if there was one?

There had been six lifeboats aboard the *Clara Nevada*, including one found down with the wreckage, one that had been deemed unserviceable, and the one found on shore with the artifacts belonging to William Hemmings and George Kasey. The Marquam investigation stated they had discovered, "parts of boats," along the shoreline, which is pretty vague. Could those parts be of one, two, or three of the other lifeboats? Did Captain Lewis use one to escape the burning ship, and if he was able to, what about any potential thieves? Was he one of them or did the thieves make off in a separate lifeboat? The ship's freight clerk, George Rogers, had oddly stayed behind in Skagway, and some believe that he did so in order to help ashore those who had stolen the gold. Another name of note from the crew was the ship's fireman, Paddy MacDonald who could very well have been the same Paddy MacDonald on the Royal Canadian Mounted Police's list of "the worst criminals known on this continent." A man like MacDonald would have had no hesitation in setting the *Clara Nevada* ablaze, and if he was posing as the ship's fireman then he would have had premium access to do so. What really happened that fateful night aboard the *Clara Nevada* we'll never know, but the story has caused many to speculate that millions of dollars-worth of gold is still out there in the cold Alaskan waters just waiting to be discovered.

Due to these types of disasters in the area, the Eldred Rock Light was approved for construction in 1905, but harsh weather postponed its opening until June 1, 1906. The oldest lighthouse in Alaska, it is the only octagonal lighthouse left in the state and is still in operation today, although it was automated back in 1973. One of the first significant sightings from the Eldred Rock

Lighthouse was, in fact, the ghost of the *Clara Nevada*, just days after the tenth anniversary of its demise its wreckage briefly pushed up onto the shore during a storm on February 10, 1908, only to be pulled back under the water by the same storm.

The man who witnessed that reappearance, assistant lighthouse keeper John "Scottie" Currie, met with his own strange fate just two years later. On the morning of March 26, 1910, he and the other assistant keeper, John Silander, set out from Eldred Rock by boat to visit the Sherman Point Lighthouse whose light was only six feet tall, to possibly assist in some sort of maintenance, although that point is unclear. While it was part of the job of the Eldred Rock keepers to tend to the minor lights of the area, Sherman Point Lighthouse was still manned at the time. After leaving Sherman Point at 12:30 PM on March 27, they sailed on and paid a visit to the town of Comet, between the two lighthouses, on their way back. They left Comet at about 4:00 PM that day with the weather reportedly fine, "with a moderate southerly wind," but the two assistants were never seen again, suddenly disappearing into the Alaska Triangle like so many others.

When his assistants hadn't returned after three days, Keeper Mils Adamson grew worried and rowed out to the *Justina Gray* to issue notice of the missing men. While a light snow had begun falling at about 9:00 PM the night of their disappearance, according to Adamson, if the two had left Comet by 4:00 PM then they should have reached Eldred Rock Light by about 8:00 PM. Two days following his report, the Eldred Rock's launch was discovered along the shore entangled in a tree and filled with water, "with all gear gone excepting mast, sail, and anchor." Adamson visited the site on March 31 and reported, "I found it to be an almost submerged tree, with long limbs under water, and, it is now my opinion that the boat sailed partly over and was capsized by this tree, the tree washed in ashore ahead of the boat thus saving the boat from being smashed." Did the tree really

Inspectors visit the Eldred Rock Light in 1906. Keeper Nils Adamson (far left), and assistant keepers Scottie Currie (fourth in row) and John Silander (far right) are pictured in front of the lighthouse.

capsize the boat and wash it up on shore? And if so, what happened to Currie, Silander, and the rest of their gear? No other evidence was ever found, their bodies remained missing, and what happened to the two assistant keepers is still a mystery to this day.

Sadly, Nils Adamson was haunted by the tragedy throughout his remaining days. According to his grandson, "He had nightmares for the rest of his life. My grandmother would sometimes find him standing in his sleep at the window shouting their names, an event that was a reprise from his days and nights alone on the rock tending the light and hoping they would be found." To this day, people claim they see the spirits of the light keepers, as well as the victims of the *Clara Nevada*, lurking about on Eldred Rock.

USS Baychimo Ghost Ship

The *USS Baychimo* was a 1300-ton cargo steamer built in Sweden in 1914 that became known as the "Ghost Ship of the Arctic" after it was abandoned in 1931 and was seen eerily creeping along the seas of northern Alaska for the next forty year s. Loaded with fur and in the middle of completing a trading run, the *Baychimo*, the largest ship ever to cross into the Arctic Circle at that time, became embedded in a pack of ice that October 1. Becoming embedded in ice was not unusual for the ship; it had happened several times before in the wintery north. Since the vessel was only a half mile from the town of Barrow (now Utqiagvik) at the time of its distress, the crew disembarked and took shelter in the town for the next two days. However, by the time the crew returned to the location where they'd left the *Baychimo*, the ship had broken free of the ice and was out floating the icy waters on its own.

The crew tried several times to retrieve their wayward vessel, at one point building a shelter near the grounded ship when it ran into another pack of ice on October 15. Over a month later, with seventeen of the crew members still living in the shelter near the cargo steamer, a terrible blizzard dislodged the *Baychimo* and it disappeared again into the snowy night. The ship was found once more by the crew, they stripped it of its cargo of valuable furs, and

One of several times the USS Baychimo *was found to be stuck in ice.*

abandoned it for good. The *Baychimo* crew believed the ship, in the condition it had become, wouldn't last the winter and would sink. Defying the odds, the old vessel from Sweden persevered for decades.

Crewless, the ghostly *Baychimo* aimlessly drifted the waters of the arctic, periodically rooting its hulk in ice and later dislodging itself to slink through the night again. Several groups of people tried to salvage the steamer over the years, but they either didn't have the right equipment or were driven back by the weather that caused her to become abandoned to begin with. One group of Alaskan Natives became trapped on the ship for 10 days when they entered the *Baychimo* and a freak snow storm suddenly hit, essentially sealing them in a frozen iron tomb. When they finally escaped, they vowed never to enter the cargo ship again, adding to the growing legends of an old ghost ship haunting the frigid waters or being powered by some otherworldly force in the great white north, cold, gray, and lifeless. Captain Hugh Polson is said to have been the final person to have boarded the ship during a salvage effort in 1939 that was, ultimately, thwarted.

The last known sighting of the *USS Baychimo* was in 1969 by a group of Native Alaskan Inuit, once again, stuck in the ice 38 years after she was first abandoned. It's unknown when she may have finally sunk or if the *Baychimo* is still out there somewhere continuing to drift. In 2006, the Alaskan government launched an extensive search for the missing vessel, but the Ghost Ship of the Arctic was never found, its lengthy disappearance just as mysterious as its prolonged survival.

Perilous Arctic Explorations

During the late 1800s, several attempts were made to navigate the Northwest Passage and to find the North Pole. Expeditions of this nature were risky, and without modern means of communication it could be years before learning the fate of many of these voyages. Thus, when the *U.S.S. Jeannette* set out from San Francisco in July 1879, one of her tasks was to determine what had happened to the Swedish *SS Vega* expedition which was thought to be lost in Alaskan waters.

Journeying from Sweden, the *Vega* and her captain, scientist and explorer Dr. Frans Reinhold Kjellman, had been trying to find the North*east* Passage and become the first to circumnavigate the Eurasian continent by sailing the Arctic Ocean and through the Bering Sea, establishing a viable route between Europe and the Pacific. This was a multi-faceted mission which also included research in geography, meteorology, and natural history of the Arctic, much of which still had not been explored as of that time. However, by the end of September 1878, the *Vega* had become trapped in ice just before reaching the Bering Strait and would remain there for nearly a year before it finally broke free. The *U.S.S. Jeannett*e would not be as fortunate.

Just less than two years after the American ship, *Jeannette*, set out on her voyage northward the ship was crushed by ice. Her

The U.S.S. Jeannette *in France setting out on her last successful voyage which would take her around Cape Horn inbound for San Francisco.*

primary mission was to reach the North Pole from the Pacific Ocean via the Bering Strait and through the same Northeast Passage the *Vega* was passing through from the opposite direction. Along the way, she was also supposed to try and discover what may have happened to Dr. Kjellman and his crew from Sweden. The *Jeannette* did make it to the Arctic Ocean, but shortly thereafter became lodged in ice on September 6, 1879, and began drifting. On January 20, the hull began leaking badly as pressure from the ice increased, but it wasn't for a full year and a half later on June 12, 1881, when the *U.S.S. Jeannette* finally sank. A handful of the crew survived and made landfall in Russia where they eventually found aid later that year.

In the meantime, the *USRC Thomas Corwin* was dispatched to find the lost *Jeannette* expedition as well as two lost whaling vessels, the *Vigilant* and the *Mount Wollaston*. If these excursions weren't so tragic with human lives lost under such brutal conditions it would be almost comedic the way the *Thomas Corwin* was out trying to find the *Jeannette* who was out trying to find the

Vega. In addition to search-and-rescue, the *Corwin* also landed several expeditions in Alaska with a scientific detail, including naturist Edward W. Nelson whose research and work from this journey we'll see in Chapter 7.

The Triangle must have been particularly feisty during this time in the late 1870s and early 1880s. While collecting artifacts and stories during their research, the crew of the *Thomas Corwin* discovered

The USRC Thomas Corwin *in the Arctic*

that the *Vigilant* had been lost in the ice with no survivors but had gone down *after* picking up survivors of the *Mount Wollaston*. Those unfortunate souls of the *Mount Wollaston* had suffered back-to-back shipwrecks. In 1882, the *Corwin* was dispatched to pick up the stranded crew of the *U.S.S. Rogers*, yet *another* ship that had been sent out in search of the *Jeannette*. This time, instead of ice, the *Rogers* caught a fire in its hold that could not be contained. Fortunately, the vessel was near enough to shore for the crew to abandon ship and set up camp, and throughout the night they watched the *Rogers* burn from the shoreline. In the morning, the fire found the ship's magazine and it exploded, sinking the vessel entirely.

The Octavius Legend

One ghost ship legend of the Alaska Triangle seems to be more rooted in myth than fact, but still warrants examination, and that's

Officers of the USRC Thomas Corwin *Arctic Relief Expedition, 1880*

the legend of the *Octavius*. The story of the *Octavius* goes back to 1761 while it sailed off to China from England with cargo to trade. The full crew along with the captain's family made it safely to their port in China, but with the weather unseasonably warm, the captain decided he would try to navigate the Octavius through the waters of the Northwest Passage which would make the return journey quite a bit shorter. When they set sail from China with their goods bound for home it was the last anyone saw them alive. When they never turned up in England, the *Octavius* was deemed lost.

In 1775, the *Herald* was working off the coast of Greenland when they happened across a derelict ship adrift in the icy waters. The captain ordered a search of the ship, and when the boarding party arrived, they were shocked at what they discovered. They found all 28 men of the crew frozen in their quarters, the expression of death chiseled permanently onto their icy faces. The captain's wife and young son were also discovered in the same condition, and the captain himself was found at his desk, ink pen frozen in hand writing out the final entry in the ship's logbook.

According to the captain's entry, the coordinates of the ship's last recorded position was just north of Barrow (now Utqiagvik), Alaska, the northern most tip of the Alaska Triangle. Terrified, the boarding party from the *Herald* abandoned the ghost ship and let it continue to drift out on the open seas. The *Octavius* was never seen again.

The story is generally considered a historic urban legend, and how much of this tale may actually be true is unknown. Author David Meyer tried tracking down the origins of the story in his online blog and discovered a possible early source for the *Octavius* in the *Gloriana*, a ghost ship story first published in 1828 in a Philadelphia-based paper named *The Ariel: A Literary and Critical Gazette*. While many of the details are eerily similar, like the dates being within a few years and the frozen crew, some details are different or entirely missing such as there being no mention of the Northwest Passage in the *Gloriana* tale. Which nuggets of the tale are true and whether this legendary tragedy really occurred in the Alaska Triangle remains to be seen.

Chapter 4

WALKING IN SHADOWS

Given the volume of work I've put together in my research on shadow entities over the years which ultimately culminated in the production of my 2020 book *A Walk In The Shadows: A Complete Guide To Shadow People*, my deep-dive shadow person workshop "Unveiling the Shadows," and my new six-part docu-series *The Shadow Dimension*, of course I've been asked to talk about reported shadow phenomena in Alaska. Have people reported witnessing shadow entities up north? Are there more of these entities than usual in the triangle area? Do these beings still look like the same shadow people we see in the Lower-48?

Shadow entities are still shadow entities, no matter where on Earth they're witnessed. That's a rather simplistic statement from me, especially given the myriad of different types of shadow phenomena there are in the known universe, and I'm not going to dive into all of those theories in this text (for an extensive look at the phenomenon of shadow entities, please refer to the aforementioned *A Walk In The Shadows* and my other work on the subject). Just know for this text there are many different types of shadow-based phenomena and, no, they're not all evil – some are simply human spirits trying to manifest into an apparition, some are interdimensional beings, and some may be extraterrestrials or even time travelers. So, yes, someone's Aunt Jane could be that shadow person witnessed at a home in Wasilla or darting down the hallway of a hotel in Anchorage.

Yes, I did see shadow entities when I was stationed in Alaska during the early 1990s ... and I wasn't the only witness. As is typically customary, I had to wait nearly a year after I first arrived at Elmendorf Air Force Base for my security clearance to be completed while the government ran around the country researching my background and talking to everyone they could find about my history and my character. For example, while I had lived my formative years in Massachusetts and Ohio, they tracked down a friend of mine in Louisiana to ask her questions about the girlfriend I had during my freshman year of high school – you know, the *real* important stuff. The amount of time and money spent to verify one's approval for a Top Secret clearance and the specific compartments I was slated for is quite astounding. While I waited for the government to learn that my first kiss was in the library at Juniper Park Elementary School and about how badly I scraped my arm making a diving catch into the visitor's dugout when I played varsity baseball, I was biding my time being thrust into a variety of computer crash courses in the squadron networking shop, running cable one moment and re-writing server subroutines originally programmed by AT&T the next. I'd become a jack-of-all trades and was learning fast a myriad of different skills that I knew would be useful for whatever IT career I might pursue later (IT wasn't really even a term back then). However, once I finally received that security clearance there was a high-percentage chance that I'd, instead, administrate messages in the base Comm Center (Communications Center). That's where the vast majority of people in my position went once their clearance came in, and it basically entailed being a glorified messenger boy –

no offense to those who actually worked the position. Besides becoming a writer and a baseball player – my first two loves – I wanted to learn computer programming, and I'd been learning some of that in the job I already held. I wanted to stay right where I'd been working.

I'd remembered the Chief Master Sergeant of the squadron telling me during my orientation that if ever there was a concern I had he had an open door to hear me out. So, I scheduled an appointment with the Chief and expressed my concerns: I didn't want to become a messenger boy; I wanted to stay with the squadron networking team. He appreciated me coming to him but informed me that the investment the government had made in me for my security clearance was a cool $100,000, so I was absolutely headed across the street. At that moment, the Senior Master Sergeant who headed up the squadron computer center which held the networking department where I worked passed by the office door and the Chief called him in to talk about my dilemma. Sergeant Schumann stated I'd been a great asset and they'd love to keep me, but he understood the situation with my clearance and would be sad to see me go when the time arrived. Chief Wann thanked him, took me by the shoulder, and walked me over to the window. He said, "I'm not just the chief over here; I'm the chief over there, too, with the WWMCCS team. Maybe I'll have you come work for me."

And, so, when my security clearance came in shortly thereafter that's exactly what I did.

I've gone through the lengths of telling this part of the story for a reason. Listen to the universe when it calls out to you and manifest what you know to be true for you. I knew the Comm Center was not going to be a good fit for me, and although I didn't get what I went to the Chief to ask for, I did end up in a position from which I gained valuable experience about a variety of technologies. Ironically, I ended up working in the same computer center that housed the Comm Center, but I knew working for that department was wrong for me and I put myself in a much better position just by simply asking. I also put myself in a much better position to witness shadow phenomena, although I had no idea at the time.

WWMCCS stood for World Wide Military Command and Control Systems, and during my time there we eventually became GCCS, or Global Command and Control Systems, although the job was essentially the same but with different equipment and software. Our team was split in two, the more administrative-oriented part of the team on the top floor of the Alaskan Command (ALCOM) building and the more systems-oriented part of the team (us) in the basement. The basement was … creepy, to say the least. Our desks were located in the back corner of a large, dimly-lit room of cubicles with our supervisor's office in the very back corner, while our communications racks were in a side room with a throughway to the very back part of the Comm Center, and our massive mainframe actually sat within the Comm Center itself with its raised subfloor.

Throughout that center, but especially in that back corner where we usually sat, something lurked. Whatever it was – or they were – was definitely shadowy in nature, many times darting behind the final partition where the extra cubicle parts were stored. Sometimes, we'd see one of these shadows dart from the room with the comm racks out the back doorway and into a small room with old servers and printers in which I'd never seen the light actually turned on the entire time I worked there. These shadows brought a dark and heavy feeling with them, but they never made any intentions known, whether sinister or otherwise. Most days, we did not see them, but there was always a dark, ominous feeling encompassing the area.

When my mother and sister came to visit during July 1995 (my father was back in Ohio breaking ground on a new house for he

ALCOM, the Colonel Everett Davis Building on Elmendorf Air Force Base (now Joint Base Elmendorf-Richardson) in January 2017. (Alvarez photo)

and my mother), I signed them in as visitors and gave them both the grand tour of the offices and the rack room. Due to security protocols, I couldn't take them into the actual Comm Center to view the mainframe. My mother, who knew nothing of the stories of the shadows which lurked within, was unnerved and completely creeped out, expressing how she definitely didn't like the feeling down in those offices.

The story circulating the facility at the time was that the building originally opened as a hospital and our offices down in that basement had been the morgue with the room where our racks stood being the location which housed the coolers. We visualized gurneys lined up across the tiled floor with cold, dead bodies on ice where our routers, multiplexors, and patch panels were stacked up and plugged in. This, however, was just fantasy and legend. I researched the history of the building and discovered that it was built for exactly what it is being used for: command. It was never a

Photo taken of the author for the squadron newsletter sometime in early 1994. The Datanet mainframe for WMCCS was housed at the back of the Comm Center. On the other side of the wall behind the Datanet is the room many said had been the "morgue," and to the left obscured by the mainframe is the doorway to the small room with old equipment in which I'd never seen the light turned on. I always got a laugh out of this photo since we never actually did anything with the floppy disks, but the photographer wanted an "in action" shot. Most of our work was either at the computer terminal to the right and out of view, in the "morgue" room with the equipment racks, or in the back offices.

hospital. So where did the story come from? As is human nature, it seems the story of the morgue was concocted to try to explain why we would have been seeing shadows and feeling dark and heavy presences where we worked.

Of course, plenty of skeptics have tried to state that the reason we were seeing and feeling what we did in the basement of that building was an effect due to the electromagnetic fields (EMF) of all the computer equipment, of which there was plenty. I understand that viewpoint, and on many investigations I've conducted I've ruled out the possibility of paranormal or supernatural activity due to high EMF. Exposure to unusually high

EMF can create a sense of dread in a person or a feeling of being watched. However, the majority of the shadow activity that was witnessed in that computer center was in the back corner of the office area where our team sat, the furthest point you could get from all of the large electronic equipment and computer mainframes. It was actually the creepiest where there was the least amount of technology present.

When it comes down to it, I can't say for sure who or what these shadows had been. Attempting to run a paranormal investigation in a Top Secret communications center to discover the origins of shadow people wasn't going to happen, not even in the back offices. The stories that were conjured up over the years were to try to make these entities out to be the souls of people who had died in a fictitious hospital. However, since that hospital never existed and the building was only ever a command center, then from where did these shadow entities originate and why were they there? Let's explore.

The Alaskan Command building was originally built as the Colonel Everett Davis building in 1947 and was viewed as the heart of Elmendorf Air Force Base. Colonel Davis was Elmendorf's first commander and first commander of the Eleventh Air Force, establishing the original Elmendorf Army Air Field in 1940. Then a Major, Davis based himself out of Merrill Field in Anchorage that August and over the next several months established a small contingent of personnel and the Elmendorf field which saw its first plane land on November 8, 1940.

Colonel Lionel H. Dunlap assumed command from Davis shortly thereafter, and Davis remained on as Chief of Staff for Colonel Dunlap and his successor in 1942, General William O. Butler. Davis was promoted to the rank of Colonel in June 1942, but he didn't get a chance to enjoy the promotion for very long. On November 28 that year, he and seven others perished in the plane crash of a C-47 out of Naknek to Elmendorf.

With such a tragic ending for Colonel Davis, the immediate question becomes … is he the one haunting the ALCOM building? Is it he that is possibly a shadow person many of us observed lurking about the computer center and offices? There's no reason to really believe this. While Colonel Davis certainly would have been rather attached to the Elmendorf base, the building built in his honor was constructed five years after his passing. He never stepped foot in it. So, what are these shadows?

Let's take into consideration that we're still within the confines of the Alaska Triangle and a vortex area of the Earth which wells up with energy from the magnetic core producing much of the strange phenomena experienced there. We've already discussed the concept that this vortex creates portals to other dimensions, which may very well be where missing vessels and aircraft, such as the Douglas C54-D we discussed in Chapter 2, disappear to. There are other ways in which these connections with other dimensions are witnessed and that is by the observation of shadow phenomena. I covered this topic using the following example in *A Walk In The Shadows*, but I'll bring it up here again for illustrative purposes. While this is an experience that happened in Oklahoma, what was observed there is pertinent to the discussion of what happened in the basement of the ALCOM building.

One of my more significant shadow person experiences lasted all of about three seconds, but its ramifications have been one of the cores of my research. A group of us were just concluding a paranormal investigation at a restaurant known as Johnny V's in Muskogee, Oklahoma, and I decided I was going to take one last photo sweep of the building. Some of the others from the team were upstairs in the bar area while others were out in the dining room when I waltzed through the main doors of the kitchen with my camera. That's when I saw it.

It was tall, narrow, translucent, and wispy. And it was so damn fast. I couldn't really say it had any significant discernible shape

The door that didn't move at Johnny V's in Muskogee, Oklahoma.

since it couldn't have been any more than six or eight inches wide, perhaps as tall as an average man, but it zipped out of there so quickly it was extremely hard to tell. From straight in front of me as I entered the room, it immediately darted to the right side of the room, and I heard it blow right through the thin, flimsy metal doors in the wall that led to the back part of the dining room. The imperative word is *heard*. The doors didn't actually move at all. What had I just seen?

I called out to the others, "Did you guys hear that?"

"Yeah!"

I questioned them on the incident, even going so far as to ask them if they had thrown something at the door in case they were trying to give me a quick jump scare. Could it have possibly been that those up in the bar, a loft-type area above the kitchen with railings overlooking the restaurant, had tossed something down that would've rattled the door? Or did the two that were out in the dining room, even though they were far in front, launch something across the room that would have slammed against the door? They hadn't, of course, and if they had thrown something at the door, I certainly would have seen it move. Made to be easy to walk in and out of the kitchen while holding large trays of food, the door was so flimsy that just barely touching it with your fingertip would have caused it to open. I certainly would have discovered whatever they may have thrown on the floor outside the door if they had done so, and I ventured through to have a look in case they really had been trying to get me to jump. There was nothing.

That the others in the group heard the same as I, it was fantastic to get that sort of confirmation, but I was able to get further confirmation of what I'd heard later when I listened back over the footage from my digital audio recorder which captured the loud banging sound. There it was, loud and clear – *bang!*

The fact that this entity blew through that door in which you could hear the sound of it but you could not see the door physically move is of great significance.

Here's what I think happened: Some sort of entity was in that kitchen when I walked in, and it was resonating as just a vague bit of shadow. When I walked in and it saw me, I scared *it* and it took off running through the door. On the shadow's plane of existence that flimsy metal door blew wide open as it ran away from me, yet I couldn't see that happen because the door remained stationary on *my* plane of existence. Yet sound is on a different wavelength and has its own frequency, so perhaps, that sound of the door being slammed into and its vibration resonated across both dimensions. While I couldn't see what actually happened on the shadow's plane of existence, I could certainly hear it. This is why I believe the missing Douglas Skymaster in Chapter 2 could have slipped through a portal into another dimension yet some radio transmissions could still be heard here – the different frequency and wavelength of the transmission could travel back through the

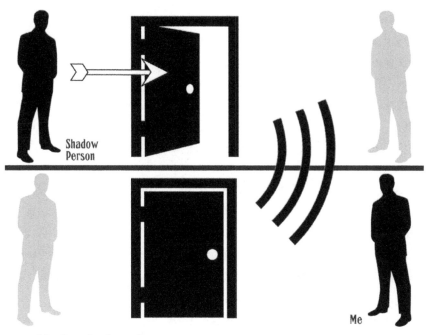

Shadow Person

Me

portal before it closed.

What I experienced – and what that shadow person experienced – in that moment happened in multiple dimensions. It happened on two different planes of existence that were overlapping each other for a short period of time. I stood, shocked, for a brief moment, the shadow entity, scared, ran off, and everyone heard the crash of the metal door. A lot of things happened in the span of about three seconds, but those three seconds have made a world of difference in the way I have viewed the supernatural – or natural – world ever since.

The adjoining illustration tries to depict this scenario with the shadow person I encountered on its own plane of existence on the top half of the diagram and my world on the bottom. You have to use a bit of imagination since this is a 2D representation of something that is at least four dimensions. The line through the middle depicts a dimensional divide, although we're really encompassing the same space, and serves as that separator between the shadow's experience and my own. That divide, however, is able to be penetrated by sound in this case, and that resonance is shown emanating from the door in the shadow's dimension and into our world. Why did it penetrate that divide this time and not every time we see a shadow person? We could postulate any number of theories, but we really don't know at this point. One other theory to consider is that these aren't really different dimensions we're looking at here as they are different points in time.

We're going to cover time travel in the Alaska Triangle in Chapter 5, but for the moment let's consider what time really is. Time is simply a human construct used to describe our reality, and it's helpful in keeping track of things like the seasons so we know when are the best times to plant and harvest crops. Oh, and your boss at work probably wants you to show up to your job at the right moment. The "river of time," however, doesn't really exist; it's just an idea we've put forth to keep track of our experience in what is really the fourth dimension. There are many who believe that all time – past, present, and future – are all happening concurrently, each moment resonating at a different frequency. However, shadow entities who are interdimensional beings are resonating on a different frequency than humans and are likely experiencing "time" differently than us.

If our personal resonance and vibration allows us to experience time in the particular fashion we usually do, i.e. 60 seconds in a minute, 60 minutes in an hour, 24 hours in a day, etc., then a being from another dimension resonating at a different frequency likely experiences time differently. Perhaps time is faster to these entities and that's why they're able to move about so quickly. Or maybe it moves slower, and when it seems to us they're standing in the corner being creepy for 20 minutes it's really more like 20 seconds to them. It's very possible time doesn't operate like a river to these beings and it's more like an elevator in which they can simply choose a floor to access a different moment. We could come up with dozens of different theories and ideas on this alone, but the point is that if shadow people resonate differently and that's why they typically reside in another dimension, then it's likely they also experience time in a different fashion. It's probably another reason why their actions seem so peculiar to us during those brief moments when we're actually able to see them.

Could the shadow entities we witnessed in the basement of the ALCOM building been an observation of a time slip powered by the Alaska Triangle? Perhaps those shadows flitting about were actually images of those personnel who had previously worked in that basement decades beforehand, shadows of real human beings living and working in another point in time. Or, perhaps, they were images of those who would come after us, some future unbeknownst to us. Could they have even been ourselves?

In a time slip, images from a past – or even future – era are observed within our own reality, including people in period clothing, structures, and wildlife with whom the observer is actually able to interact. One of the more well-known stories of this kind is the Versailles Time Slip in 1901 in which two middle-aged English women, Eleanor Jourdain and Charlotte "Annie" Moberly, were walking through the gardens of the Palace of Versailles when they suddenly noticed that the other people around them were dressed very differently and quite similar to those during the Eighteenth Century prior to the French Revolution. These people included a pockmarked man on the step of a summerhouse, as if he'd contracted small pox and a woman in an Eighteenth Century gown drawing a sketch of Marie Antionette. In addition to the people, they also spotted a plough in the garden although there hadn't been a plough present since the reign of King Louis XVI.

Can shadow people be observations of time slips? Can the shadows we see possibly be images from another time and place starting to manifest in our own plane of existence but don't completely take shape?

At the Historic Anchorage Hotel in downtown Anchorage, Alaska, there have been reports of the shadowy silhouette of a woman from a bygone era who appears throughout the building. There are plenty of other hauntings at this location which we'll cover elsewhere in this book, but the fact that there's enough of an image of this person that manifests, albeit more shadow than apparition, that witnesses can tell it's a woman is interesting. The same is true of the dark shadowy entity at the Red Onion Saloon in Skagway which many believe is the spirit of a bouncer who once worked there by the name of John. Is the energy from the Alaska Triangle empowering these locations enough to kick off a periodic time slip between our point in time and theirs? Are there other locations within the triangle area that have reported this type of phenomenon? We'll cover time travel phenomena more extensively in Chapter 5.

What I want to avoid here is to simply describe shadow phenomena experienced during paranormal investigations in Alaska and hauntings throughout the region since we'll talk more about hauntings later. What's interesting to me is how the energy of the region affects this type of activity and actually encourages it to manifest. What are these different manifestations and appearances by these entities?

Shadow entities can be a variety of different things, and to examine all of those possibilities is beyond the scope of this book. I covered these topics extensively in my book *A Walk In The Shadows: A Complete Guide To Shadow People*, as shown above with my description of what happened at Johnny V's, but let's look at some basics.

Human Spirits – Many shadow entities are simply human spirits who haven't collected enough energy to manifest as a full-bodied apparition.

Extraterrestrials – Some shadow beings are likely extraterrestrials from other worlds or traveling here interdimensionally. There are several similarities between the way people report shadow encounters and the way they report encounters with ETs.

Interdimensional Beings – This is what I believe a "true" shadow person is, something that has entered our reality from some other plane of existence. There may be some crossover here with extraterrestrials or the next one in the list.

Time Travelers – I talked about this above and will talk about it more in the next chapter. If not an intentional time traveler, a shadow entity could be an unintentional time slip.

Tulpa – Basis of the "thought form" from early Buddhist texts literally meaning *manifestation*, the concept that a sentient being can be created from your thoughts. For example, Walter B. Gibson writing *The Shadow* pulp novels under the pen name Maxwell Grant is said to have created a shadow tulpa in the house where he penned his novels.

Astral Projections – Partial physical manifestation of the energy of someone who has projected their consciousness out of their body.

Light Beings – Higher dimensional being whose pure energy is in a light wave form beyond what the human eye can comprehend, thus we only see a silhouette.

Agent of a Simulated Universe – If the universe we live in is a simulation, what would that make shadow people within the simulation? An observer collecting data? Some sort of "game master" interacting with and controlling the environment? An agent reminiscent of those in *The Matrix* movies?

Something we still don't yet know – I always leave this door open since there's still so much about this universe we don't yet understand.

In *The Shadow Dimension* docu-series mentioned back in Chapter 1, we researched and investigated specific locations which reported significant shadow phenomena that we also suspected to be powered by vortex energy. These were small sample sizes –

"The Conjuring House" in Harrisville, Rhode Island in which *The Conjuring* movie was based and Mineral Springs Hotel in Alton, Illinois, right on the Mississippi River down the road from Cahokia Mounds which includes the largest pyramid north of Mesoamerica. The Conjuring House is seemingly powered by the little powerhouse of a room in the basement which includes an open well filled with water and limestone walls capped with granite. The Mineral Springs Hotel is caught between the water and the limestone bluffs and still has the massive hole in the sub-basement where the old spring had been tapped into. Both are rife with shadow and other supernatural activity. If these two smaller locations are teeming with shadow activity based on the magnitude of the energy of the land, then how much more active with this type of phenomena is a region like the vast and energetically volatile Alaska Triangle?

Chapter 5

SOMEWHERE IN TIME

Time travel is an extremely popular topic in our world today and is used as a plot device in many of our science fiction and fantasy books, films, and television shows. In fact, my all-time favorite television show as of this writing, the German-produced *Dark*, is all about time travel and unusual paradoxes. While this concept makes for great story telling while simultaneously challenging the mind, does time travel really exist?

I touched on a few of these concepts while talking about shadow people in Chapter 4, and while I won't get too heavy-handed in the details, let's dive into this a little further. I had written previously about time being a human concept, that the "river of time" is, essentially, just an illusion. Shadow people may just be a time slip when frequencies resonate together in the right fashion, yes, but how might that work?

Those who have been following my work for several years will be familiar with something I've called the *stacked time theory*. I'm going to cover this more in depth in my upcoming book *Connecting The Universe*, but I want to at least provide some basics about it here for the conversation. Imagine, if you will, that every moment that ever has occurred, is occurring, and will occur in a specific location are all stacked together in one extremely tall pile of photographs – a living picture captured every second, if you will. All these captured photos are still living and on-going within that tall stack without knowledge that the others in the stack are also living and on-going. The time slips we previously talked about would be when two of these moments in the stack of photos resonate at the same frequency and overlap for a moment. Time travel would be the ability to go to a location and move up and down this stack of moments at will.

Explaining Stacked Time Theory using a stack of photographs for a video blog on the Haunted Road Media YouTube channel in 2015.

During my years of research, although I formulated this theory on my own, I've come to realize that this idea has many similarities to Albert Einstein's theories about the space-time continuum. What influenced me to jump down this rabbit hole, however – no offense to Einstein – was the aforementioned film industry. Ever since I was a young kid in the early 1980s, I've loved the movie *Somewhere In Time,* starring Christopher Reeve and Jane Seymour, based on the novel *Bid Time Return* by Richard Matheson. In this heartbreaking story, Reeve's character has journeyed to a hotel on Mackinac Island where he is drawn to the historic portrait of a beautiful woman. He desires to meet her and wills his consciousness from 1980 back to 1912. In order to do this, he acquires clothes and other items from the era to use the power of his mind and convince himself in his 1980 hotel room that he is actually at the hotel in 1912 at the exact same time the woman is there. With his consciousness, he was able to jump from one photo in the Mackinac Island stack to another. I believe when we finally discover the secrets of time travel it will be more of this nature, rather than something mechanical, to make these journeys. Time travel will have more to do with meditation, the interconnections of the universe, and consciousness than a Delorean and a flux capacitor. We'll also be able to use the Earth's energy and sites of power around the globe to aid us in these meditations and take us on these journeys as they may have once done so in ancient times.

All of that said, what does that have to do with the Alaska Triangle? Part of the Alaska Triangle does cut through Canada's Yukon Territory and a remarkable time travel proposition was offered to the public concerning that area in November 2019. A photograph taken along Dominion Creek in 1898 suddenly went viral on the Internet as a girl shown in the photo looked remarkably similar to young, modern-day Swedish environmental activist Greta Thunberg. Is Miss Thunberg a time traveler gone back to try to address climate issues before they reached the level of today's concerns? As of this writing, she has yet to comment on the photograph, but intense speculation took the Internet by storm for a short while.

The photograph in question was discovered in the archives of the University of Washington which digitized its collection in 1997. However, facial recognition technology hadn't found widespread use until recent years, and it's possible someone stumbled upon the Dominion Creek photo while running an image search on Thunberg. The original collection of photographs taken

Three children operating a rocker at a gold mine on Dominion Creek, Yukon Territory, ca. 1898 Photograph: Eric Hegg/University of Washington Libraries

by Swedish American Eric Hegg was donated to the university more than 50 years before it suddenly became a social media sensation, and those previously familiar with the photo were more amazed at how involved children had become in the process of mining for gold during that era.

Much like other gold rushes, prospectors and families flocked to the Klondike area when it was discovered there in 1898, but most particularly the Dominion Creek area which has produced over 20 million ounces of gold since that time. Eric Hegg had been one of those prospectors, although he never struck it big; however, being a photographer by trade, he sought to capture the lives of those people hoping to discover the richest of the north.

None of the children in the famed photograph are named, so it's unknown who they truly were. Is there any possibility that the girl in the forefront of the photograph is really Greta Thurnberg, or is this just a case of celebrity look-a-like more than 120 years

Greta Thunberg attends in the European Economic and Social Committee event in 2019. The resemblance to the Dominion Creek photo is uncanny.

apart? Additionally, what is the strange being leaning on the ground behind the children on the left side of the photograph? Whatever it is, it's an unusual aspect of the photo that often gets overlooked while most people are concerned with the appearance of the girl.

There is precedent for this sort of phenomenon. Not far off the beaten path in British Columbia, the South Forks Bridge in Gold Bridge reopened in 1941 after it had been washed away during a flood the previous year. During the festivities, a photographer captured an image of the onlookers that included a man who looked determinedly out of place. He wore a logo shirt that many believe appears silk-screened, wrap-around sunglasses, and he carried a small, portable camera. What a time traveler may have been doing at the South Forks Bridge reopening, we have no idea, but he definitely didn't resemble people typical of the era. Since the discovery of this photograph, he's become known as the "time traveling hipster."

The "time travelling hipster" wearing wrap-around sunglasses at the South Forks Bridge reopening, ca. 1941 Photograph: Bralorne Museum

The photo is authentic, originating from the Bralorne Museum in central British Columbia, and it suddenly went viral online in spring 2010 as part of the Virtual Museum of Canada from the Canadian Heritage Information Network. The sudden surge in traffic from the internet and massive interest in the photograph came as a complete surprise to the network.

Skeptics against the man in question being a time traveler state the following reasons for his unusual appearance: The logo on his shirt resembles that of the Montreal Maroons hockey team that existed in the old National Hockey League for fourteen years from 1924 – 1938 (although this would have had to have been some sort of alternate uniform that saw limited use). Sunglasses with protective sides, while not widely available, did actually exist in the 1940s. And, portable cameras from Kodak were also on the market in 1941, although again, they may not have been widely available.

So, was this man really a time traveler, randomly captured on camera by a photographer at the South Forks Bridge, or was he just a man with a fashion sense ahead of his time in 1941? We'll never know for sure. On a side note, I've joked around during conference presentations that this man resembles my good friend and co-star on *The Alaska Triangle* television show, Jonny Enoch, who just also happens to be Canadian.

These are fun photos that may have some sort of reasonable explanation as to how they came to be – or they might not – but at this point they provide us with some food for thought about the possibilities of real time travel and how that would look. Are there ways to consciously move through space and time in today's day and age, and how would that be powered? If it's just a matter of slipping into another place in time through the power of the mind or the energy of the body, would standing in a highly energetic location like the Alaska Triangle aid in making that happen and give the process a boost, so to speak?

Previously, we discussed the missing Douglas Skymaster airplane in 1950 that possibly disappeared into a portal created by the vortex energy of the Alaska Triangle. If that truly happened, where did the airplane go? Did it disappear into some sort of parallel universe or did it suddenly find itself in another time, some other year?

If it did pass through a portal to some other point in time, perhaps into the past, we could have heard about its fate long ago through unexpected means. There are accounts and legends of strange sky phenomena within our ancient cultures that may give us clues to the reappearance of these craft in a different period of time and a far different culture. We'll explore some of those possibilities throughout this book, but if that's the case, then these would be moments in which something from the future influenced the past, a potential result of traversing time, whether that's through my stacked time theory or some other means. If so, significant paradoxes could already be woven within the fabric of our very existence.

Do we have an account of this kind of time travel of an airplane into a portal in which we could talk to the pilot afterward to learn more about what exactly happens during this phenomenon? While not in the Alaska Triangle, we can examine the strange experience of Bruce Gernon in the Bermuda Triangle which may be similar.

In 1970, pilot Bruce Gernon flew into what he ended up calling an "electronic fog" in the Bermuda Triangle and traveled forward 30 minutes in time. Flying from Andros Island to Ft. Lauderdale, a flight Gernon routinely made, massive dark clouds formed up ahead of Gernon's plane and morphed into a spiral which swallowed the craft into some sort of tunnel. The plane's instruments began malfunctioning as bright white flashes illuminated the sky, and he feared for his life. Fortunately, Gernon came out on the other side of the tunnel unscathed; however, the city of Miami, surprisingly, was below him. Gernon was happy to be alive but was completely perplexed. With the city staring at him out the window it meant he'd traveled 100 miles in three minutes!

Bruce Gernon's experience is just one of many of the strange occurrences that has happened in this area of the world, and he was fortunate enough to have survived, but was it really survival or just that he somehow managed to navigate his aircraft well enough to keep it in this timeframe – or even this dimension?

His description of the clouds forming into a spiral could be similar to what the crew of the missing Douglas Skymaster airplane experienced in 1950. In addition to Gernon's experience, British Wing Commander J. Baldwin flew into a cloud during the Korean War never to be seen again even after the other pilots in the formation scoured the area for him. Where *or when* did he go? If the Douglas Skymaster slipped into another point in time, we may not see it again until years and years from now in the future, or it could even be hidden under layers of ice from hundreds of

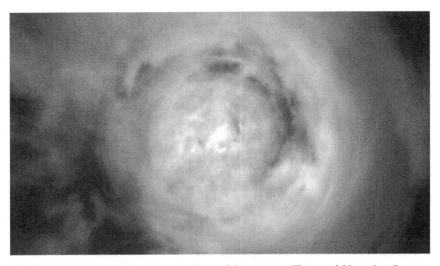

Swirling clouds creating a type of tunnel formation. This could be what Bruce Gernon or the crew on the Douglas Skymaster witnessed.

years ago in the past. Is it possible that some of the thunderbird legends from indigenous peoples from long ago were actually sightings of airplanes that had traveled in time through a portal created by the vortex energy of the Alaska Triangle? We'll explore that idea more in Chapter 7.

Are some of the reported missing person cases around the state actually cases of time travel? How many of the 16,000 people who have gone missing in Alaska since 1988 aren't really missing at all and just traveled to another point in time? Bizarre disappearances occur all the time in Alaska. In 2012, runner Michael LeMaitre disappeared right in the middle of the Mount Marathon race in Seward. Along with all the other racers in the run, LeMaitre had ventured 1.5 miles up the mountain, but he never came back down. An extensive search of the area revealed nothing.

Former police officer and investigator David Paulides has done a fantastic job researching and cataloguing a bevy of strange missing persons cases in his *Missing 411* series, accounts of people disappearing off the face of the Earth out in the wilderness, many of which are right next to other people while hiking together out in these remote areas. For an extensive dive down this rabbit hole, I highly recommend taking a look at his work. I also recommend if you have information about a missing person in Alaska to contact the Alaska Missing Persons Clearinghouse[6], an organization that was assembled to aid in the overabundance the state has of these types of cases.

Rather than occurring right next to a person on a path out in the woods, sometimes these types of disappearances happen right in front of people's eyes. In the vicinity of the Dragon Triangle in 1964, the Japanese newspaper *Mainichi* reported the disappearance of an automobile on a crowded highway. Witnesses included three officials from the Fuji Bank who spotted an elderly man in the back seat reading a newspaper as they were driving outside of Kanamachi. According to the *Mainichi* account, "Suddenly, a puff of something gaseous, like white smoke or vapor, gushed from somewhere around the black car, and when this cloud dispersed (a matter of not more than five seconds), the black car had vanished." Was this the same type of smoke or cloud Bruce Gernon had witnessed in the Bermuda Triangle or the squadron of planes in Korea or even the Douglas Skymaster?

In 1930, near the Alaska Triangle in Canada, an entire Inuit village suddenly disappeared. Of the village's 30 inhabitants, all suddenly went missing, leaving behind their food, clothing, kayaks, and rifles. Everything that would have been essential to their survival in the bleak wilderness they left behind in the village – and not a footprint or track had been left in the snow. The discoverer of this abandoned village, a fur trapper named Joe Labelle, had stumbled into the village looking for refuge on a cold, bitter night. The people of the village couldn't have been gone long – Joe found a pot of stew still cooking, although what was in the bottom of the pot had charred and was smoking.

Labelle stated afterward, "I felt immediately that something was wrong ... In view of half cooked dishes, I knew they had been

---

[6] Visit https://dps.alaska.gov/AST/SAR/MissingPerson

disturbed during the preparation of dinner. In every cabin, I found a rifle leaning beside the door and no Eskimo goes anywhere without his gun ... I understood that something terrible had happened."

Alarmed, Labelle trudged back through the snow to the nearest telegraph office and had a message sent to the Canadian Mounted Police who ventured out to investigate. Their findings were disturbing. The village burial ground had been desecrated, every single grave unearthed and the bodies removed. An entire pack of sled dogs was discovered just outside the village starved to death and buried beneath the snow. The Mounties had also seen a mysterious blue glowing light that night, much different and stronger than the typical Northern Lights of the region, pulsating on the horizon.

Where did the inhabitants of this village disappear to? Did they really leave everything behind and just walk away from their homes, without leaving footprints, somehow? Or did they, perhaps, experience the vortex energy of the Triangle welling up from the Earth's magnetic core to send them to another dimension or another place in time? Some would suggest the blue glowing light was reminiscent of UFO activity.

There is some controversy to this story as Joe Labelle had just received his trapping license that season, and his report of previously encountering this village with 2,000 inhabitants has been called into question. The conservative number of 30 used above is the reported number by journalist John Keel in his book *Our Haunted Planet*. Whichever the case, the disappearance into thin air of a substantial number of people in quite unusual.

There are also cases in which people disappear and then reappear having experienced large moments of missing time. We often hear about these types of experiences when people recount UFO abduction cases. The missing time in many of these stories is usually chalked up to a memory wipe while the abductee is with

Do "little people" from another dimension in space-time live within the great mountains of the Alaska Triangle?

the extraterrestrials or as a way for the mind to deal with the trauma of what had happened. Either of these could certainly be true, especially the latter. What if one of the reasons for the missing time is that the ETs took the abductee to another dimension, another place in space-time in which time works differently, and in coming back to Earth the time displacement from the other dimension doesn't quite match with Earth time. That would certainly be a form of time travel, and we have already seen what scientists call *gravitational time dilation* to a small degree when astronauts travel to and from space. Although it's very slight, those that spend time on the International Space Station actually age at a lesser rate than those on Earth.

A strange story came out of Marshall, Alaska, in 2008 when a hunter encountered a young boy out in the woods that May who seemingly appeared out of nowhere. As reported in the *Anchorage Daily News* on June 1, 2008, the boy was disoriented and confused without any real sense or concept of time, and what's more is there were no tracks in the snow surrounding him. How did he get there? In time, the boy revealed he'd been brought inside Pilcher Mountain where he was questioned by "little beings" that are known as the ircenrraat (pronounced irr-chin-hhak) to the indigenous peoples of the region. There, he also met a little girl who had been abducted over 40 years ago, but she had not aged. Time seemed to stand still or operate differently within this location. After spending some time with the girl, the ircenrraat decided to release the boy, and that's when he appeared in the snow where the hunter found him.

In a much earlier account that doesn't actually involve irregularities in time, Edward W. Nelson published a story in 1899 about these beings in which villagers encountered a very small man and woman with a child. From "The Dwarf People" in *The Eskimo About Bering Strait*:

> *The old people were about two cubits high and the boy not over the length of one's forearm. Though he was so small, the man was dragging a sled much larger than those used by the villagers, and he had on it a heavy load of various articles.*

We'll see more of Nelson's work later in the chapter on cryptid encounters, but it's interesting to note here that these small beings seemed to also possess some sort of unusual, perhaps even supernatural, strength. These types of entities are reported in cultures from all around the world in a variety of forms, whether they're called little people, gnomes, dwarves, fairies, or other terms, and their special abilities varies from region to region. Some believe tales of these beings may even be stories about extraterrestrials told in the context and understanding of the humans at that time. Perhaps.

Much of the lore of these types of beings involves accessing other realms and dimensions, traveling to our world using some sort of gateway or portal. Going beyond the lore and looking at this through a scientific or technological lens, then perhaps these entities have mastered space-time, figuring out how, if time is all concurrent, to take themselves outside of time and access whichever moment they wished.

Could they be living in or have access to what many have defined as a tesseract, a physical representation of the fifth dimension (not the Marvel magic cube). The Merriam-Webster dictionary defines tesseract as "the four-dimensional analogue of a cube," although when discussing dimensions, the first dimension is a line, the second a plane, the third a cube, the fourth is time (where we exist). The tesseract is a means to look at time much in the same way as we look at a three-dimensional object. For reference, Matthew McConaughey's character in the film *Interstellar* gets trapped in one of these and is able to view the physical representation of every moment in time of his daughter's bedroom.

Ancient and indigenous cultures discussed these concepts through a different modality. Instead of submitting scientific research papers to peer-reviewed journals, they explored the inner-workings of the universe through spirituality and myth. Inside all legends and lore, however, are the seeds of truth. Are there "little people" out there who have mastered space and time, and are they abducting children for years, sometimes decades, at a time with seemingly no passage of age? If some race of entities has discovered a dimension in which immortality like that has been mastered, then the Alaska Triangle may be one of the doorways there.

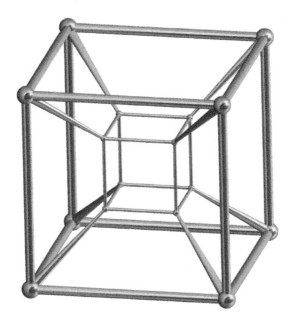

Schlegel diagram of a tesseract[7], essentially a cube on top of a cube in our human attempt to conceptualize what one would actually look like.

[7] Created by Robert Webb and his Stella software package:
http://www.software3d.com/stella

Chapter 6

EXTRATERRESTRIALS

On June 25, 2021, the United States government, through the Office of the Director of National Intelligence (ODNI), released a widely anticipated report on Unidentified Aerial Phenomena (UAP). Many had hoped this report would, once and for all, give full disclosure from the government about UFO and extraterrestrial activity that has been occurring for decades on our world. Instead, the report landed with a resounding thud.

In a brief nine-page paper (the classified version is, reportedly, 17 pages long although some have said it may be 70 or more pages in length), the ODNI blandly stated under a section titled "UAP Probably Lack A Single Explanation," "With the exception of the one instance where we determined with high confidence that the reported UAP was airborne clutter, specifically a deflating balloon, we currently lack sufficient information in our dataset to attribute incidents to specific explanations."

This was one of a series of vague statements throughout the report, that also included such gems like:

"We currently lack data to indicate any UAP are part of a

foreign collection program or indicative of a major technological advancement by a potential adversary."

"These observations could be the result of sensor errors, spoofing, or observer misperception and require additional rigorous analysis."

"... there was wide variability in the reports and the dataset is currently too limited to allow for detailed trend or pattern analysis ..."

"The limited amount of high-quality reporting on unidentified aerial phenomena (UAP) hampers our ability to draw firm conclusions about the nature or intent of UAP."

Even more disappointing is that, *"this report is currently limited primarily to U.S. Government reporting of incidents occurring from November 2004 to March 2021,"* completely ignoring the previous 57 years of research and analysis carried out by, not only individuals and organizations in the private sector, but also the government, itself. That the report makes this statement, *"No standardized reporting mechanism existed until the Navy established one in March 2019. The Air Force subsequently adopted that mechanism in November 2020, but it remains limited to USG reporting,"* is disheartening considering the significant military involvement in these studies in the past.

Project Blue Book was a government operation (primarily U.S. Air Force) studying reports of UFO sightings from 1952 to 1969, preceded by Operation Grudge (1949 – 1951) and Operation Sign (1947 – 1949). During Blue Book's run and the research of the renowned Dr. J. Allen Hynek, the project compiled 12,618 reports, 701 of which are still unexplained and remain open to this day.

That the recent UAP report completely ignored these open cases and is overtly vague on what the report does actually cover is a massive disservice to real research in the area of unexplained aerial phenomena.

Fifty-seven years beforehand, a report from Project Sign on August 4, 1947, stated that Captain Jack Peck and co-pilot Vince Daly witnessed and followed a "flying saucer" northwest of Bethel, Alaska, around sunset. This was just nearly a month after the infamous Roswell, New Mexico, incident. According to the initial filed report:

> *"The object, which appeared as large or larger in mass than a C-54 and black in color appeared silhouetted against a brilliant evening sky. In order to avoid a possible collision (being unable at first to determine in what direction the object was moving) they pulled up to about 1200 ft in order to avoid a possible collision. The object crossed their path at right angle to them. Seeing that it was moving away from them at a very rapid rate and flying at an altitude from 500 to 1,000 ft they swung in behind it and followed it an at air speed of 170 MPH but the thing was out of sight in four minutes. They state that the object was smooth surfaced and streamlined and resembled a C-54 without motors (from the rear) and was without wings or any visible means of propulsion whatever. Wind was negligible and it was on a NW course.*
>
> *Official in Charge of the Airlines for which Peck was working states that the pilot is not of the 'imaginative type.'"*

Following up on this report, the T/4 Signal Corp Operator in Charge, Harold D. Johnson, forwarded a report titled "Matters of National Interest" to "Commanding Officer, Alaska

Communication System" which stated much of the same from above and then added:

> *"It is realized that the Fourth Air Force claims there are no such things but Captain Peck is Chief Pilot for Al Jones flying services and is not a man given to exaggeration. In view of the excellent reputation of Captain Peck and the fact that no one there doubts the least but that he actually saw this object, this report is turned in for any action deemed necessary by your office."*

This is just one of many early reports for which we're left with no explanation and the recent UAP report won't even touch. Why is it that our society has the propensity to withhold information, or spread disinformation, that hurts or prevents our own progress?

On the night of January 22 – 23, 1950, just three days before the Douglas Skymaster airplane we discussed in Chapter 2 went missing in the Alaska Triangle near Snag, there was a significant UFO sighting near Kodiak in the area of the Bering Sea. At 2:40 AM that morning a strange radar reading was taken by a Navy patrol pilot but quickly vanished. He reported the reading to the Kodiak station and inquired if there were any other aircraft in the area. When Kodiak responded that there were no other aircraft in the area of the Navy pilot, *they* reported they were having strange interference problems.

Twenty minutes later just south of Kodiak aboard the *USS Tillamook*, an officer on deck reported seeing, "a very fast-moving red glow light, which appeared to be exhaust in nature." In a clockwise fashion, the strange light circled the Kodiak area, originating from the southeast and returning from whence it came after it circled. Another officer came out on deck during this time and also witnessed the phenomenon, describing it as, "a large ball of orange fire."

Kodiak Naval Air Station, winter of 1949 - 1950

At 4:40 AM, two hours after the first sighting, the Navy patrol pilot again saw strange activity on his radar. The blip his equipment caught moved so fast that it left a trail of light on his radar screen. The pilot called his crew who suddenly witnessed the UFO zoom five miles in ten seconds at a speed of about 1,800 miles per hour. He tried to pursue but was absolutely no match for the speeding object which suddenly turned abruptly and headed straight toward his airplane. The UFO zipped by and was never seen again. Other witnesses during this final incident described the object as two orange lights that rotated around a center point between them.

While not directly in the Alaska Triangle area – the exact boundaries are elusive and more of a guide anyway – it's a significant event to note since it directly preceded the missing aircraft just three days later. Was the UFO activity in the early morning hours of January 23 a prelude of things to come?

For the Navy, it seemed to be a fairly significant event since they distributed 36 copies of their report to various security agencies – such as the FBI and CIA – around the country. In his book *UFOs and the National Security State: Chronology of a Cover-up 1941 – 1973*, Richard M. Dolan made the following observations:

> *[Captain Edward] Ruppelt [of Project Blue Book fame] claimed that UFO investigations at this time rated "minimum effort." The old Project Grudge files, he said, had been "chucked into an old storage case," and many reports were missing when he sifted through them a few years later. What, then, of the Kodiak case? We do not know the military's response to this, but Ruppelt noted that early in 1950, the director of Air Force intelligence (one of the recipients of the Kodiak report) sent a letter to ATIC [Air Technical Intelligence Center] indicating that he had never issued any order to end Project Grudge. ATIC replied weakly that it had not actually disbanded Grudge but merely transferred its project functions and no longer considered it a special project. It is possible that the Kodiak incident sparked this exchange.*

Kodiak Naval Air Station, winter of 1949 - 1950

Mysterious UFO sightings at Kodiak resurfaced on September 26, 2007, when several on the island witnessed something falling from the sky. Some described bright lights while others reported some sort of plane or other craft burning as it fell and crashed into the island. Strangely, despite a significant search-and-rescue effort, there was no reported crash and no further words came from officials. It was as if nothing ever happened.

In January 1965 there seemed to be a flurry of UFO sightings around Anchorage in which the local newspapers documented, "a rash of reports from people telling of unexplained things in the sky," which included, "strange flying devices and brilliant lights." The January 27, 1965, edition of the *Fairbanks Daily News-Miner* quoted a Mrs. Ed Ray from Anchorage as witnessing, "a noise 'like a buzzing sound' – just before the lights appeared.

'Suddenly it was just blinding,' she said. 'It was high – we all looked up – coming down into the trees. Then it flashed through the house and just before it went out the kitchen window there seemed to be an explosion, or flare, of great intensity. It was brighter than looking right into a 1,000-watt bulb. We thought there might have been an explosion.'"

A spokesman at the time for the University of Alaska Geophysical Institute chalked up the sightings to, "auroral activities in the past week which may have caused optical illusions." Auroral activities, however, don't usually burn as bright as a 1,000-watt lightbulb, nor do they usually involve a buzzing sound.

Since I spent three years in Alaska during my service in the U.S. Air Force, I often get asked if I have any UFO secrets to share from the great white north. Did I witness anything? Did I have access to UFO research? Are there UFOs hidden at Elmendorf Air Force Base? Did Air Force personnel talk about UFOs? Of all of those questions (and there are plenty more), only the latter could I give an affirmative. There was certainly some chatter amongst personnel about UFOs, but that's really about all it amounted to.

If there was significant UFO activity happening in Alaska that the Air Force was involved with, I wasn't a part of that, and even with a Top Secret security clearance, I didn't have a "need to know." That doesn't mean UFO activity didn't exist there and that people didn't talk about Unidentified Flying Objects (UAP wasn't a term back then, it was all UFO), people most certainly did. But I didn't have any means at my disposal while I was there to substantiate anything anyone ever said. So, as of this writing, I can't give you any juicy personal Air Force UFO encounter stories while I was stationed there in Alaska from 1992 – 1995. That said, there are still plenty of encounters with UFOs and UAPs that have been reported by others in Alaska for several decades.

JAL Flight 1628

The most documented UFO case in Alaska involved Japan Airlines Flight 1628, a cargo flight out of Paris to Reykjavik, Alaska, and then on to Tokyo on November 17, 1986. The captain, Kenju Terauchi, was an ex-fighter pilot and had more than 10,000 hours of flight time over 29 years as a senior airline pilot. By all accounts, he was a stand-up airline captain. Yet, about 104 miles northeast of Fort Yukon in the skies of the Alaska Triangle, Terauchi spotted unidentified lights out the left window below the plane.

Captain Terauchi with a drawing of the UFO he witnessed.

At first, he disregarded these lights believing they may have been military aircraft, but after a few minutes he realized the lights were actually pacing Flight 1628. Terauchi radioed the Anchorage Air Route Traffic Control Center and asked about other possible aircraft in the area. The Anchorage Control Center reported that there was no military aircraft in the vicinity and ground radar only showed Flight 1628 in that area. The lights Terauchi witnessed then began moving erratically.

According to the captain's own account:

The distance from the lights was far enough from us and we felt no immediate danger. I thought, perhaps, it was a UFO. The lights were still moving strangely. Most unexpectedly, two spaceships appeared [directly in front of the plane], shooting off lights. The inside cockpit shined brightly and I felt [the warmth of the UFO's thrusters] on my face.

Then, three to seven seconds later, the fire – like from jet engines – stopped and became a small circle of lights as they began to fly in level flight at the same speed as we were. The middle of the body of the ship sparked on occasional stream of lights, like a charcoal fire. Its shape was a square, flying 500 feet to 1,000 feet in front of us, very slightly higher in altitude than us. Its size was about the same size as the body of a DC-8.

It is impossible for any manmade machine to make a sudden appearance in front of a jumbo jet that is flying 910 kilometers per hour and to move along in a formation paralleling our aircraft. But we did not feel threatened or in danger. Honestly, we were simply astounded. I have no idea why they came so close to us.

There was a pale white flat light in the direction where the ships flew away, [pacing us]. The Anchorage Center replied that they saw nothing on their radar. I set our digital weather radar distance to 20 miles, radar angle to horizon. There it was, on the screen: a large, green, round object had appeared seven or eight miles away in the direction of the object.

We arrived at the sky above the Eielson Air Force Base and Fairbanks. It was a clear night. We were just above the bright city lights and we checked the pale white light behind us. There was a silhouette of a gigantic spaceship! We must get away quickly!

Terauchi attempted evasive maneuvers to try to shake off the mysterious craft, including flying in circles and changing altitude, but through it all the UFO continued to shadow Flight 1628. Anchorage Center offered to scramble a military jet, but fearing a military confrontation might endanger the lives of his crew, Terauchi declined. A few minutes later, a United Airlines passenger jet flew into the same air space and was requested by the Anchorage Air Route Traffic Control Center to get a visual on the situation, but then the UFO disappeared into thin air never to be seen again after following Flight 1628 for more than 400 miles.

About a week later, Federal Aviation Administration (FAA) Division Chief John Callahan of the Accidents and Investigations Branch in Washington D.C. was suddenly thrust into the situation when the Alaska media created a frenzy over Flight 1628's chase.

According to Callahan in a 2000 interview:

I forgot who it was that called, but he says, 'We got a problem here. I don't know what to tell the media. The whole [FAA] office is full of the media from Alaska.

I told him to get all that data together. I wanted all the [civilian and military] disks that they had and all the tapes that they had available — and flown overnight to the tech

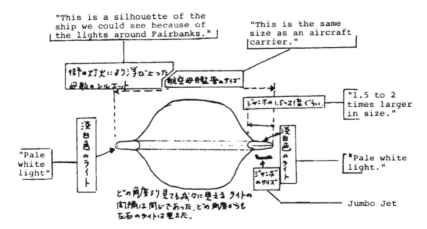

Captain Terauchi's drawing a month and a half after the incident.

center where I'm sitting. The military refused to send their tapes, but he got everything Anchorage Traffic Control had.

Callahan recreated the entire setup of the night of the incident, tying all elements together, including the radar, the digital radar, and the sound. When his recreation setup was complete, he heard a three-way conversation between Anchorage Air Traffic Control (ATC), Elmendorf Air Force Base's NORAD Regional Operations Control Center (ROCC), and Captain Terauchi of JAL Flight 1628 while viewing the tapes of the ATC radar scope. While Anchorage Air Traffic Control didn't have a visual of the UFOs on their radar, Callahan believed the conversation indicated the Air Force had been tracking the objects.

Callahan continued in the interview:

Details reported by the military controller indicated that the UFOs were traveling thousands of miles per hour as they maneuvered in the airspace around the 747. The military controller had one other surprise finding. Near the end of the incident a United Airlines flight was diverted to observe the JAL flight. By then, Captain Terauchi no longer saw the huge UFO, and the United pilot did not see it either. Unbeknownst to both of them, the military radar clearly indicated that the UFO had tucked in out of sight behind the United Flight and had begun following it.

The FAA assembled a briefing so Callahan could report his findings to the FBI, the CIA, and a scientific study team from the Reagan Administration, along with several others. All those present were excited about the report Callahan presented, but he was ordered not to say anything about it to anyone outside those at the briefing under the premise that the news would cause widespread panic throughout the country.

Callahan additionally stated, "When they asked me what I thought, I told them that it looked like we had a UFO that was up there. As far as I was concerned, Reagan's science team were the ones that verified my own thoughts about it. They were very, very excited about the data. They had said at that time that this was the was the only time — and they had used the words 'a UFO' — was ever recorded on radar for any length of time."

On March 5, 1987, the FAA released their formal findings at a press conference, retracting previous statements that the controllers had confirmed a UFO sighting and declaring, "the FAA [did] not have enough material to confirm that something was there," and while they were, "accepting the descriptions by the crew," the FAA was, "unable to support what they saw."

Ironically, while the JAL Flight 1628 investigation was still in progress, on January 29, 1987, there was another UFO sighting by Alaska Airlines Flight 53 about 60 miles west of McGrath, Alaska, as it traveled from Nome to Anchorage. The object was beyond the range of the Anchorage Air Route Traffic Control Center, but in a certified transcript from the AARTCC, the pilot reported seeing an object on radar, "moving about a mile a second," and suddenly, "just disappear in a matter of seconds."

A report filed by the FAA stated the following:

At approximately 1835 AST the crew noticed a return on the weather radar at their 12 o'clock position and at a range of 25 miles. Both pilots stated that the target was strong and bright. They both looked outside and could not see any lights or targets. Looking back at the radar the target had moved approximately 5 miles further ahead of them to approximately 30 miles. Each sweep of the radar (approximately 1 second) the target would move 5 miles further ahead of them until it went off the radar scope at 50 miles.

The controller on duty checked with the USAF (Alaska Air Command) and was told they did not have aircraft operating in that area at that time.

The very next day, a U.S. Air Force KC-135 pilot flying from Anchorage to Fairbanks spotted a large, disk-shaped object only about 40 feet from his aircraft. Little is known about this incident, likely because it was military, and in the AARTCC transcript the pilot was told to, "give them a call after you land at Eielson [Air Force Base]." We have no idea what was discussed in that call.

Unidentified Submerged Objects (USOs)

UFOs and UAPs aren't just witnessed over land, however. Sometimes, they are also witnessed in and emerging out of our planet's waters. Instead of calling them UFOs, these craft are identified as USOs, or Unidentified Submerged Objects. These types of extraterrestrial vehicles, like their airborne counterparts, have been spotted all over the world, and they may indicate there are some sort of ET bases hidden beneath the Earth's watery depths. Given the sheer amount of unexplored territory under our oceans – we've only explored, approximately, five percent – the possibilities of what's hidden beneath the water is staggering. Alaska, alone, has over 46,000 miles of tidal shoreline[8] – more than all the "lower 48" states combined – and contains more than three million lakes over 20 acres large, encompassing more than 40% of the nation's surface water, which leaves plenty of space for USOs to slip in and out virtually undetected.

The first such one of these craft witnessed in the area of the Alaska Triangle may very well have happened in 1943 while World War II was in full swing. The *USS Williamson*, a naval destroyer, was patrolling near the Bering Sea in April just after supporting an occupation of the Aleutian Islands of Kiska and Attu. At about 11:00 PM on the night of the possible USO incident, crewmembers spotted a row of red lights off the port side of the ship flying parallel with the *Williamson* and only about 100 yards away.

One member of the crew from the starboard side stated, "I did not see the lights when they first approached so I do not know the direction from which they came, or if they came out of the sea. There were at least eight lights in a row, evenly spaced, canted at about 15 degrees to horizontal."

The red lights flew silently about 10 feet apart from each other and about 30 feet above the water, pacing the ship for nearly an hour until they finally disappeared. Where did they go? Were the lights some sort of extraterrestrial craft, and did they possibly return to some sort of base underneath the ocean?

---

[8] Reported by the Alaska ShoreZone Coastal Inventory and Mapping Project in partnership with the National Oceanic and Atmospheric Administration.

Artist's interpretation of a UFO over the water in the Arctic.

A couple years later in the summer of 1945 near the Aleutian Islands, 14 sailors aboard the *USAT Delarof*, a U.S. Army transport ship, were amazed when they witnessed a large, dark sphere rise up out of the ocean, circle their transport, and then zip off away from them in a curved trajectory.

The National Investigations Committee on Aerial Phenomena (NICAP), formed in 1956 to study this type of activity and headed by Donald Keyhoe from 1957 – 1969, reported the following which can be found on their website[9]:

The ship, heading back to Seattle, was in the open sea past Adak. It was about sunset, and [Robert S.] Crawford [who served as a radio operator aboard the Delarof*] was on the port side near the radio room when he heard shouts from some of the crew. He turned and saw a large, round object which had just emerged from the sea. (Several crewmen saw the UFO actually appear from underwater, an estimated mile or so from the* Delarof.*) The unknown craft, showing darkly against the setting sun, climbed almost straight up for a few moments, then it arced into level flight, and began to circle the ship. All the observers were convinced it*

---

[9] http://www.nicap.org/reports/45SUMRaleutianisles_waterufo.net_item.php_id=49.pdf

was a large object. Comparing it with the width of a finger held out at arm's length, Crawford estimated the UFO to be 150 to 250 feet in diameter. As it circled the Delarof, *the flying object was in easy range of the ship's guns. But the gun crews held their fire, though on the alert for any sign of hostility. The UFO circled the vessel two or three times, moving smoothly and with no audible sound. All the witnesses felt it was self-propelled; otherwise, the strong winds would have visibly affected its movements. After several minutes, the flying object disappeared to the south or south-southwest. Suddenly the crew saw three flashes of light from the area where it had vanished. The* Delarof *captain posted an extra watch as the ship moved through that sector later, but nothing was seen. At Seattle, 14 crewmen signed a summary of the sighting.*

Crawford, the radio operator aboard the *Delarof*, later became a geology consultant at the Indiana Soil Testing Laboratory at Griffith, Indiana. Aside from his account which he shared with NICAP consultant and Professor of Geology N.N. Kohanowski, there appears to no additional follow up to this early report.

In 1969, U.S. Navy high speed code operator Dan Willis working at the San Francisco Naval Communications Center received a strange message in Morse code from a ship off the Alaskan coast. The fact it came in via Morse code relayed through a communications site on Skaggs Island raised a reg flag since, by that time, Morse was only used as backup ship-to-shore communications when bad atmospheric conditions distorted standard radio methods. The message stated that the vessel's crew had spotted a brightly glowing reddish-orange elliptical object, perhaps about 70 feet in diameter, rise up out of the water and shoot off into space. The ship's radar picked up on the object and recorded it racing into the stratosphere at speeds up to 7000 Miles per hour. Considered a top priority message when it came in, the

Artist's interpretation of an Unidentified Submerged Object (USO)

report seems to have been buried, and documents on this incident have yet to be released.

Why might extraterrestrial beings find building underwater bases in Alaska, if they exist, to be so attractive? First and foremost, the chance of humans discovering a base underwater is significantly reduced since less than 20% of the global seafloor has actually been mapped[10]. According to the National Oceanic and Atmospheric Administration (NOAA), "While almost 50% of the seafloor beneath U.S. waters had been mapped to these modern standards, the nation's seafloor is larger than the land area of all 50 states, the District of Columbia, and the five territories combined. Thus, there's still a significant amount of seafloor left to be mapped at high resolution." That's a lot of water in which to hide.

Extraterrestrial craft may also be using Alaska's electromagnetic activity to power up their vessels, harnessing the Earth's energy like a giant battery pack. We previously discussed

---

[10] Using multibeam high-resolution sonar systems, according to NOAA.

the volatility in that part of the world between earthquakes, volcanoes, and more. On July 28, 2021, an 8.2 magnitude quake hit 56 miles off the coast of Perryville, Alaska, along the Alaska Peninsula which stretches out into the Aleutian Islands. Tsunami warnings were issued but later canceled. A week later, three volcanoes in the Aleutians began erupting simultaneously. That's a lot of energy exploding out of the Earth in a short period of time.

The entire arctic region, in general with its extreme isolation, may be of great interest to extraterrestrial visitors. In their May 2015 issue, French conspiracy magazine *Top Secret* published photos from an anonymous source that were supposed to have been taken during a 1971 excursion through the Arctic by the *USS Trepang*, a U.S. nuclear submarine. The images are said to have been captured far off the east coast of Greenland, between Iceland and Jan Mayen, an island controlled by Norway and used by their meteorological institute.

These photographs are controversial, and I was not able to secure the rights to publish them here, but during the seventh episode of *The Alaska Triangle* television show, MUFON investigator Jeremy Ray described what the photos depicted:

> *The images look like a massive craft has ascended out of the water and hovered for a little while for the Navy guys to take pictures of it. It's like a cylindrical saucer, but oval-shaped object that you can see in the photographs when it's coming out of the water the water's still falling off the craft. Then the object turned sideways, [and] from the report, took off at a high rate of speed.*

Unidentified Submerged Objects are still prevalent throughout the Alaska Triangle today. There have been several accounts from passengers on cruise lines touring throughout the area who have reported seeing dancing lights in the sky, around the ship, and along the waters. Over Memorial Day weekend 2010 while fishing out in the Prince William Sound, the crew of a charter was blown away by a rumbling sound out of the southwest that swelled to the northwest and lasted six minutes. And witnesses at Smitty's Cove, 60 miles from Anchorage in the Whittier area, have stated they've seen thousands of extraterrestrial ships rise up out of the water.

Remote Viewing Mount Hayes

View of Mount Hayes from the South (Bureau of Land Management photo)

Rising to an elevation of nearly 14,000 feet (13,832) and looming near the geographical center of the Alaska Triangle is one of the highest peaks in the United States in Mount Hayes. While standing tall and proud in the Alaska Range and adorned with a significant glacier, Mt. Hayes has taken on additional prominence as a possible hot spot for extraterrestrial activity. How could that be at a location as remote and treacherous as Hayes is? There's no road one can take to the slopes of the mountain. One must fly to

Mt. Hayes and land on the glacier (a local bush pilot can help with that if one is so inclined), and UFOlogist James Fox did just that on *The Alaska Triangle* television show.

The motivation for investigating possible activity at Mt. Hayes has its roots back in Project Star Gate, government research initiatives involving psychic abilities, primarily remote viewing. Although controversial, these viewing sessions and experiments were part of the intelligence gathering methods the United States utilized during the Cold War, primarily targeting the Soviet Union. Transcripts of Star Gate-based meetings revealed military concerns that, "One of our problems is keeping track of the Russians," and that the results of these tests had the vested interest of the Oval Office. From the minutes of a 1979 project meeting at Fort George G. Meade: "Did Congressman [Charlie] Rose tell you that he went to the White House and spoke to the President about this and the President is still interested?"

The President of the United States at that time was Jimmy Carter, a man who had openly admitted to witnessing UFO activity when he was a younger man in 1969. Carter was somewhat skeptical about remote viewing, but was open to its potential as long as it worked. In one particular incident, a Soviet airplane, a Tupolev-22 bomber, had gone down somewhere in Zaire, Africa. It would be a big win for the United States if they could find the plane and search through it for valuable information, but U.S. spy satellites couldn't find the wreckage. It was as if the dense African jungle had swallowed the plane whole. Enter Project Star Gate – or Grill Flame as it was called at that time (Star Gate was the name given in 1993 to encompass all of the remote viewing programs over the previous two decades). After being given a photo of a Tu-22, remote viewer Frances Bryan was told a similar plane had gone down in Africa and needed to be found. Bryan produced an overhead sketch of the area with the jungle and a river, and with the coordinates she gave, the plane was found within three miles.

In President Carter's own words, "She went in a trance, and she wrote down latitudes and longitudes, and we sent our satellite over that latitude and longitude, and there was the plane."

The mission of the Star Gate programs had been as follows:

To establish a program using psychoenergetics for intelligence applications. Specifically, utilizing that field of psychoenergetics referred to as REMOTE VIEWING. The program encompasses the following:

- *Establishing a training program in REMOTE VIEWING utilizing selected INSCOM [Intelligence and Security Command] personnel.*
- *Establishing procedures for intelligence collection techniques utilizing REMOTE VIEWING.*
- *Establishing a mechanism for responding to intelligence collection requirements (tasking) using REMOTE VIEWING.*

While remote viewing extraterrestrial bases was not a primary objective of Star Gate projects, it was an occasional byproduct of the process. The man who viewed the activity occurring at Mount Hayes in Alaska was Pat Price.

Pat Price was a remote viewer who once served as a local councilman for Burbank, California, and also spent some time as police commissioner where he put his

Pat Price

psychic and remote viewing abilities to work. He was semi-retired and raising Christmas trees when his life took an unexpected turn and he became involved in Project Star Gate at the Stanford Research Institute in 1973. A few years beforehand he had met Hal Puthoff, the director of the CIA/DIA-funded program, at a lecture in Los Angeles, and by chance, Puthoff and fellow remote viewer Ingo Swann ran into Price while he was selling the trees at a lot in late 1972. After a brief conversation, Puthoff gave Price his phone number which Price used that following June after he became concerned about receiving an increasing number of psychic impressions about people and wanted answers. During the course of conversation, Puthoff tested Price on coordinates given to him by a CIA analyst. Price began detailing an installation hidden in the mountains and additionally mailed Puthoff several pages of sketches and other documents describing what he had seen while he viewed the location. The documents were so on point describing a secret Navy communications site filled with NSA cryptographers that when Puthoff passed the documents along, a brief investigation was launched into the matter interrogating those involved as to how they got inside the installation. While the test had caused quite a stir, Price was now aboard the Star Gate project.

During his stint on the program, Price walked into Puthoff's office one day in 1973 and dropped a folder on his desk. "You might be interested in these," he told Puthoff.

Inside the folder was information on four UFO bases Price had remote viewed on his own with descriptions of their locations and functions. These locations included Mount Perdido in the Pyrnees Mountains between France and Spain, Mount Inyangani in Zimbabwe, Mount Ziel in Australia's Northern Territory, and Mount Hayes in Alaska.

Regarding Mount Hayes, Price's report described the site as a type of weather and geological center. His viewing session revealed computer equipment, oscilloscopes, and a small box-like component with a rotational antenna mounted on top of the mountain peak and appeared to be part of some sort of detection system for atmospheric monitoring. The base bore deep underground and contained super-advanced humanoids, differing in heart, lungs, blood, and eyes working side-by-side with humans, likely military personnel. Price's report also stated, "This site has also been responsible for strange activity and malfunction of U.S. and Soviet space projects."

Tragically, Pat Price served only a brief tenure in Stanford Research Institute's program and died under mysterious circumstances in July 1975. The CIA had moved Price to their own facilities in the Washington D.C. area in April of that year, and a day after meeting with the Office of Naval Intelligence and the National Security Agency, Price died in bizarre fashion in a Las Vegas hotel room. Some say the death was natural, some say the KGB killed him, and yet others say the CIA was involved. Whichever the case, following dinner, Price began convulsing in bed, and at one point he convulsed so severely that his body arced to the point that only his head and feet were touching the bed like something out of a demon possession movie. His breathing was described as sounding like a "death rattle" and then stopped entirely. Paramedics were too late to the scene to help. While his body was rushed to the hospital, there was no autopsy performed and his body was cremated before his wife was even called about the matter. Mysterious circumstances, indeed.

In the years following Price's death, Star Gate projects took up a more formal residence at Fort Meade in Maryland, the same home as NSA, until 1995 when it was disbanded (ironically, just months before I arrived there as a young airman). Price's folder concerning UFO installations passed from Hal Puthoff to Skip Atwater in the early 1980s, with Puthoff uttering Price's same words, "You might be interested in these."

In time, Atwater gave remote viewer Joe McMoneagle the challenge target of Alaska's Mount Hayes. Although he didn't definitively state precisely what the function of the installation was, what he saw was still quite interesting:

> *I've never seen anything like it. It's like walking into a place I have no familiarity with at all. It's not just something you describe. It's all brand new. There's a desolate open range of mountains. ... The whole thing is underground and is powered by like an atomic power plant. ... This is a prototype of something. I don't get an aggressive nature to this target.*

> *All of the drawings and comments support a number of probable possibilities. One is underground UFO Bases. The other is an Over-the-Horizon Radar site. Another would be some other form of system like the HAARP which is still classified.*

The controversial High Frequency Active Auroral Research Program (HAARP) Array is about 100 miles southeast of Mount Hayes. Is the location of HAARP due to the remoteness of Alaska or is it possibly utilizing some of the electromagnetic properties of the Alaska Triangle? That's beyond the scope of the UFO discussion, but it's food for thought, and we'll come back to it.

A couple years later, Atwater gave the same Mount Hayes target to remote viewer Mel Riley. According to a document dated January 28, 1987, and titled "Description of Personnel Associated 'ET' Bases," Riley's notes stated:

> *MT. HAYES ... There appeared to be two types of entities associated with this site. The two entities located outside of the structure were accomplishing some sort of routine task ... unable to make contact with them or gain information of any sort. Inside the structure were two*

SG1J

28 JANUARY 1987

DESCRIPTION OF PERSONNEL ASSOCIATED "E.T" BASES

So far have run into three types of entities associated with bases at various locations within the solar system.

TITAN BASE..... all personnel observed at this base on 20 November 1986 appeared to be no different than native earthlings. There were two male technician-types sitting at a control panel of some kind. Behind them stood an attractive female with brown shoulder-length hair, wearing a pale green lab coat or smock. She appeared to be in some sort of supervisory role.

MT. HAYES....... there appeared to be two types of entities associated with this site. The two entities located outside of the structure were accomplishing some sort of routine task....unable to make contact with them or gain information of any sort. Inside the structure were two entities....one sitting at some sort of circular console with a round screen-like object. The other was busy doing something in the background. The entity at the console appeared to be human in form, but lacked definitive facial features. He seemed friendly enough and invited me to observe his actions at the console.

SOUTH AMERICA/AFRICA....... there appeared to be two types of entities associated with this site also. The first had a very large, round-shaped head on a slender neck....very unhuman in appearance....almost robot-like ....unable to make any contact with this being. The other entity was almost human-like in appearance. His face was devoid of any hair, his complexion was very pale.... facial features were very indistinct with the exception of a sharp, slender nose. This entity seemed friendly enough and appeared to

CIA document now missing from the FOIA Reading Room.

entities ... one sitting at some sort of circular console with a round screen-like object. The other was busy doing something in the background. The entity at the console appeared to be human in form, but lacked definitive facial features. He seemed friendly enough and invited me to observe his actions at the console.

Interesting to note, as of this writing, the direct link to the online CIA archives with the handwritten note[11] is no longer active and forwards one to the default Freedom of Information Act Reading Room. If one puts in the document name into the search bar there, CIA-RDP96-00789R003800110001-8.pdf, a message is returned that simply states, "Failed to Load PDF Document." Is this just a server glitch or has this document been removed for some other reason?

I was able to find the file, however, on the trusty archive.org Internet Archive at link: https://archive.org/details/CIA-RDP96-00789R003800110001-8.

Over the decades there have been several UFO sightings reported around the Fort Greely area and nearby Delta Junction just 38 miles from Mount Hayes. One memorable object sighting was in 1957 which, at one point, was thought to be a rocket from Russia's Sputnik satellite. It was reported to have landed in the vicinity, but after several days of searching it was deemed unidentifiable after the investigation could not locate the object that fell from the sky. More conventional sightings included four military police on the fort in 2008 who witnessed three green circular lights on the underbelly of something triangular in nature. They reported the sighting to their supervisor who dismissed the incident as an airplane. Green lights were witnessed at Fort Greely again in 2009. Lights have also been witnessed over time in the skies above Delta Junction, but these colors seem to be more orange in nature.

---

[11] https://www.cia.gov/library/readingroom/docs/CIA-RDP96-00789R003800110001-8.pdf

CRYPTID ENCOUNTERS

Cryptozoology, as defined by the Miriam-Webster dictionary, is, "the study of and search for animals and especially legendary animals (such as Sasquatch) usually in order to evaluate the possibility of their existence." The Alaska Triangle is loaded with these types of legendary creatures, but to include all of the various types of cryptid encounters in Alaska would take far too much paper. There are tomes filled with accounts of these creatures, such as David Weatherly's *Monsters of the Last Frontier*, but I do want to include some of the more important ones here.

Thunderbirds

There are several variations to the indigenous legends of thunderbirds throughout the Americas, and the Alaskan native cultures have theirs as well. Thunderbirds are said to be massively large winged creatures with supernatural powers primarily related to storms. These huge birds with wingspans up to dozens of feet are said to have created thunder with their wings and lightning shot out from their eyes when they blinked. Pictographs around the continent often depict thunderbirds with outstretched wings, prominent feathers, and zig-zag lines representing the lightning they bore. These stories of massive birds permeate throughout Tlingit and Inuit cultures with many legendary accounts concerning thunderbirds hunting whales. Much like an osprey swooping down to the ocean and snatching a fish, thunderbirds are said to essentially do the same with whales, swooping down and snatching them out of the water. Sometimes, they may even snatch an entire canoe, human included.

Edward W. Nelson was a young naturalist in his early 20s when he ventured to Alaska in 1877 and studied native culture and the surrounding habitat. As part of the U.S. Army Signal Corps in search of the lost *Jeannette* expedition (see Chapter 3), he spent the next four years there deeply embedded in the local flora and fauna, Inuit culture, their beliefs, and collecting artifacts.

Edward W. Nelson in Alaska

In his extensive work on Alaskan life titled *The Eskimo About Bering Strait*, Nelson recounts the tale "The Last of the Thunderbirds":

> *Very long ago there were many giant eagles or thunderbirds living in the mountains, but they all disappeared except a single pair which made their home on the mountain top overlooking the Yukon river near Sabotnisky. The top of this mountain was round, and the eagles had hollowed out a great basin on the summit which they used for their nest, around the edges of which was a rocky rim from which they could look down upon the large village near the water's edge.*

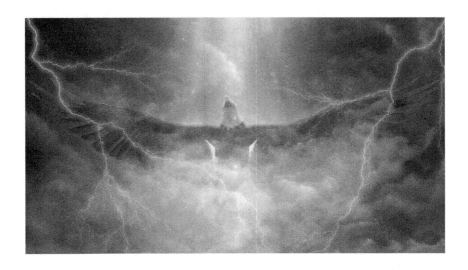

From their perch on this rocky wall these great birds would soar away on their broad wings, looking like a cloud in the sky, sometimes to seize a reindeer from some passing herd to bring back to their young; again they would circle out, with a noise like thunder from their shaking wings, and descend upon a fisherman in his canoe on the surface of the river, carrying man and canoe to the top of the mountain. There the man would be eaten by the young thunderbirds and the canoe would lie bleaching among the bones and other refuse scattered along the border of the nest.

The story continues and tells the tale of a young hunter who kills the last of the thunderbirds after his wife had been snatched and flown to the nest to be eaten. While the tale may seem like pure myth to some, there apparently had been physical evidence from which the story was derived. A footnote included in Nelson's account states:

The truth of this tale is implicitly believed by the Eskimo of the lower Yukon. They point out the crater of an old volcano as the nest of the giant eagles, and say that the ribs of old canoes and curiously colored stones carried there by the birds may still be seen about the rim of the nest. This is one of the various legends of the giant eagles or thunderbirds that are familiar to the Eskimo of the Yukon and to those of Bering strait and Kotzebue sound.

There's precedent for large birds in days of old. The largest flying bird on record, the *Argentavis magnificens*, or Giant Teratorn, had a wingspan of 5.8 – 8 meters (19 – 26 feet) with a body length of about 3.5 meters (11.5 feet). However, these birds lived back in the Miocene epoch about 6 million years ago, so these likely are not our thunderbirds unless, by chance, a scant few managed to survive the ever-changing planet and its myriad of cataclysms over that time. The wandering albatross (*Diomedea exulans*) is our current largest flying bird with a wingspan of about 3.7 meters (12.1 feet), probably a bit smaller than traditional thunderbird legends. Albatrosses also don't shoot lightning out of their eyes, and likely, neither did the Giant Teratorn.

I have another theory regarding thunderbirds and what may have influenced the indigenous peoples in their telling of these origin stories containing thunder and lighting. Let's revisit the missing Douglas Skymaster airplane from Chapter 2 and we'll again ask, if this airplane did disappear into a portal, where did it go? If it did find itself in another place in time much more extensively than Bruce Gernon's experience in the Bermuda Triangle, where was that other point in time? Could it have jumped into the far past, say … 500 years ago? If it possibly did, what would a massive Douglas Skymaster look like to the indigenous peoples of the far north at that time? They would have had no concept of what an airplane is. But something extremely large flying through the air with a wide wingspan and extremely loud sounds emanating from it … how would they perceive that? Is it possible some of our missing airplanes lost through portals which took them back in time could have become some of the thunderbird legends of old? Were the indigenous peoples just describing modern technology they witnessed in the only context they knew at that time? It's certainly worth considering.

Giants in Alaska

Cultures all over the globe have legends of giants, whether that's the Nephilim of the Bible, Goliath, the giants' tombs of Sardinia, the giants living on Easter Island when it was first discovered by Europeans in 1722, giants in the Solomon Islands that some claim still roam today, and the plethora of giant bones discovered throughout America that have perplexingly gone missing over the past 150 years. Our past is screaming out to us that extremely tall humanoid people did, in fact, roam this planet.

Recent discoveries of Denisovan remains in Siberia of a young girl from 75,000 years ago showed that these hominins did, generally, have larger features, including teeth found in Tibet so large they were originally mistaken as belonging to a bear, and were taller than modern human beings, but scientists are hesitant to approximate a height for these peoples. Cautioning against these

Denisovan mandible with two massive molars. (Dongju Zhang photo)

estimations, Gabriel Renaud, bioinformatician at the University of Copenhagen, stated, "If you were to find a single *Homo sapiens* fossil and it's an NBA basketball player, then you might conclude that *Homo sapiens* were seven feet tall. ... We can't verify the predictions until several Denisovan skeletons are found."

While that's a prudent statement to make, one can't help but to make connections from the Denisovans to accounts of giants in Alaska. In 1937, Alaskan Inuit native Michael Francis Kazingnuk began writing out by hand what would become a 500-page tome on the history and traditions of his people. This work, *The Eskimo[12] History Story*, is a highly valued piece of work that is now housed by the Alaska State Library and was transcribed by the Kawerak Social Science Program. Amongst the plethora of stories Kazingnuk compiled were ones of giants, some with connections back to Siberia across the sea. While the English in this work is broken and choppy, it's insightful to the traditions of the northern indigenous peoples and the history they passed down through the ages.

And, there were giants borned by human being
Two in the Bering Sea Coast at Siberian,
One in Indian point village, his name was
  Angkatungunna, 10ft.
He got killed in Big Diomede Island, by good
  man Ayakhak.

There are more than ten feet height those giants.
And one in Yong range Siberian Coast.
His name was Nan-khies-Kan.

---

[12] The word "Eskimo" is now widely considered unacceptable by Alaska Natives since it was a name assigned to them by non-indigenous peoples, but it was the term Kazingnuk used in his work since that was the common word for his people at that time.

This giant has six slave servants young
and strong Chuckchis men.
He was a cruel to so many of his neighbors
in around the coast.
Finally, he got killed by his slave servants.

And six were giants or more in around the Alaska.
These brothers giants in Buckland Alaska.
Oldish one was his name Kuop-ruppuk.
Younger one his name was Ella-Khunic.
Third younger one his name was Peelak.
Later, them two oldish giant brothers killed this
younger brother Peelak.
Because he was wicked and desperado about the
human being peoples.
When this happen is over, those two brothers were
beginning to hunt and killed kind of useless
bad wild animals and wild games.
Killed as many they could found there in the Sea and
in the Land. So that those human being won't feared
of them.

Also, two more giants there were around in the
Port Clarance Alaska.
First one his name was Ak-see-soo-kak.
he lived around in Cape Douglas, and his cousin
his name was. Plee-Ta KaLowak.
he lived around in old Marys Egloo Alaska.
Both of them was great helpful to human being people.

Also, one giant was in the St. Lawrence Island.
He was keep helping to his people around there in
his time.

Those giants raise no children,
    because they have no female of their own,
    to raise some children and to make their
    own populations and race.

In this illustration we see accounts of three giants coming from Siberia: *Two in the Bering Sea Coast at Siberian* and one who was specifically named and more than ten feet tall, *There are more than ten feet height those giants. And one in Yong range Siberian Coast. His name was Nan-khies-Kan.* At this time, we can't say definitively if these were Denisovans or decedents thereof, but it's certainly worth looking into. We also see some possible Nephilim connections littered throughout: *And, there were giants borned by human being* as well as *Those giants raise no children, because they have no female of their own.* Thus, we see interbreeding between a giant race of people and humans, much like we see in the Bible's book of Genesis and the Book of Enoch.

Genesis 6:4 (NIV):
    The Nephilim [in some translations 'giants'] were on the earth in those days—and also afterward—when the sons of God went to the daughters of humans and had children by them. They were the heroes of old, men of renown.

1 Enoch 9:8-9:
    They have gone in to the daughters of men of earth, and have lain with them, and have defiled themselves with the women. ... And now, look, the daughters of men have borne sons from them, giants, half-breeds.

This isn't to say that the giants described in Kazingnuk's writings were actually Nephilim, but it's possible they could have been descended from them over millennia. They could also be the legendary tornits, or Alaskan "bushmen" who are said to have crossed the Bering land bridge long ago. In 1901, the Bulletin of the American Museum of Natural History published the following in Volume 15:

In early times the Tornit, a race of very large people, inhabited the country. They quarreled with the Eskimo because the latter intruded upon their land. This made the Tornit angry, who broke the ground with their lances and spears, and split rocks into pieces. It is believed that the Tornit and Ijiqan, both races of giants, inhabit the interior.

What's interesting to me about this passage is the relative age of the tornits, predating the Inuit by quite some time. How long, we don't know for sure, but the first wave of humans that are to have crossed over the Bering land bridge are believed to have done so about 15,000 years ago during the Ice Age when sea levels were lower. At that time, these peoples would have been cut off from access to the south as the massive Cordilleran and Laurentide Ice Sheets, one mass covering most of the northern half of North America at that time, would have stood in their way. So, if there were already large hominins in the area, where did they come from? Did the giants cross the land bridge before *Homo sapiens* or did they migrate from the south at another point in time?

For decades, there was a "Clovis First" mentality when remnants of early human activity was discovered near Clovis, New Mexico, in the early Twentieth Century and were believed to be the original progenitors of Native Americans. This school of thought proposed that about 14,100 years ago global warming reduced the ice sheets and allowed humans to migrate south throughout the Americas, eventually settling the "Clovis" culture that lasted from 13,400 years ago to 12,800 years ago when they suddenly disappeared. However, at Monte Verde in southern Chile in 1977, Tom Dillehay, Professor of Anthropology at Vanderbilt University in Tennessee, found evidence of human activity dating as far back as 18,500 years ago, a few thousand years before humans were said to have crossed the Bering land bridge and a good 5,000 years before the Clovis culture was established.

These findings were met with harsh criticism, but over the next 40 years more discoveries would be made showing us that our human past in America is much older than we originally believed. A site in Pennsylvania known as Meadowcroft, about 27 miles southwest of Pittsburgh was discovered to have evidence of human occupation dating back 19,000 years. Then right on the edge of the Alaska Triangle in the 1990s, Canadian archaeologist Jacques Cinq-Mars excavated the Bluefish Caves in Yukon Territory near Old Crow and found the presence of human activity there as far back as 24,000 years ago. More recently, Tom Deméré, Curator of Paleontology at the San Diego Natural History Museum, published a paper in the April 27, 2017, edition of peer-reviewed journal *Nature* announcing the discovery of an archaeological site in southern California with a human presence dating back approximately 130,000 years.

With so many gaps in the timeline dating back so far into history, there's a lot more we need to discover first before we can determine where these giants may have come from. Did they travel across the Bering land bridge? Did they travel across the ocean hundreds of thousands of years ago and disembark in South America or the southern California area, fanning out across the Americas? In a recent episode of our *Edge of the Rabbit Hole* livestream show[13], we discussed giants with author and researcher James Keenan who has extensively researched the unusual

---

[13] Skinwalkers, Giants, UFOs, and Mysteries of the Uintah Basin with James Keenan streamed September 7, 2021 on the Edge of the Rabbit Hole YouTube channel: https://www.youtube.com/watch?v=leyHYciJWws

phenomena in and around the Uintah Basin in Utah and believes many of America's giants originated in the Uintah mountains and migrated outward from there into other parts of the continent. Whatever the origin point may have been, what would have attracted these beings to migrate so far north into the Alaska Triangle? Was the electromagnetism of the area, the earth energy, such a strong draw for them?

According to Aztec mythology, the giant known as Xelhua, one of seven who survived the Great Flood, built the pyramid of Cholula and the city of Teotihuacán in what is now Mexico. These giants, or Quinametzin, were said to have once populated the world and, as seems to be a recurring theme throughout world cultures, were punished with the flood by the gods for the sins they had committed. Could some of these giants migrating out from Uintah, pre- or post-flood (like Xelhua), have traveled northward and, like the construction of Cholula and Teotihuacán, have built Alaska's Black Pyramid we'll see in Chapter 10, tapping into the earth energy like we see so many other pyramidal structures around the world do?

Physical giant evidence has been discovered over the years, but where it is today is anyone's guess, and many believe it's been purposely hidden. In November 1900, newspapers around the country disseminated a report out of Atlin, Alaska, that gold miners had discovered a

SKELETONS OF GIANTS IN ALASKA

Ancient Cemetery Uncovered in the Atlin Gold District.

Special Dispatch to The Call.

VANCOUVER, Nov. 17.—James L. Perkinson, an American miner of Atlin, arrived here to-day with news of the finding of a number of skeletons in an ancient Indian cemetery in the north, which is of startling scientific interest. Perkinson is one of the owners of the Yellow Jacket, a rich claim which is supposed to be the fountain head of Pine, the principal creek in Atlin district. Two weeks ago the first excavations were being made for a new tunnel on the property and what appears to have been an old Indian burying ground was opened up.

Article on the Atlin giants, 1900.

153

number of skeletons at the Yellow Jacket mine belonging to prehistoric giants nearly seven feet in height and one that was actually more than seven feet tall. Explorer Hugh Newman, who appeared on *The Alaska Triangle* television show, and co-author Jim Vieira published a snippet of a newspaper article and the accompanying Smithsonian Institute record in their book *Giants On Record* of the find of a massive human skull discovered in the Aleutian Islands in 1936. This skull was 2,005 cubic centimeters when the average adult human skull is about 1,400 cubic centimeters. The Smithsonian records show the skull was checked in on February 4, 1937, but it has since gone missing. The disappearance of giant remains is, unfortunately, a common theme throughout the country making this line of research much more difficult than it ought to be.

Sasquatch and Hairy Man

A discussion about giants naturally leads one into a discussion about Sasquatch, Big Foot, or the Skunk Ape, various names for the same type of creature depending on which area of the country you're in. Alaska also has a being known as the Hairy Man.

Port Chatham, a bay with an abandoned village of the same name, lies on the southern tip of the Kenai Peninsula south of Anchorage. The town is also sometimes referred to as Portlock after British sea captain Nathaniel Portlock who sailed there in 1786, and has become home to one of Alaska's strangest legends – the Hairy Man. The town was once home to a rather successful and thriving salmon cannery, and later a chromite mine, in the early Twentieth Century, but the town was later abandoned under seemingly mysterious circumstances.

The town had a natural eeriness to it with a fog that routinely rolled in off the bay and would hang thick in the trees. The

The cannery at Port Chatham in 1909

roaming indigenous Sugpiaq peoples of Russian-Aleut descent who worked at the cannery had their own legends of the Nantiinaq, pronounced 'non-tee-nuck,' a Sasquatch-type creature that was half-man, half-beast, who roamed the forest. One didn't want to get caught in the fog with the Nantiinaq lurking about. Non-Natives eventually called this creature the Hairy Man.

The first reported incident of something unusual in the surrounding forest came in 1905 when all the Native workers at the cannery suddenly evacuated the entire area, completely. It wasn't until the following year when they returned. Throughout the 1920s and 1930s there were several reports of a large, man-like beast roaming around the forest, and although it wouldn't usually come into the village or around the cannery, some who ventured into woods alone would meet an untimely death. In one particular incident, a man named Albert Petka is said to have scared off the Hairy Man with his dogs, but in the process suffered a massive blow to the chest by the creature that ultimately killed him.

In the 1940s the stories of the Hairy Man started to pick up with shocking tales of bodies washing up on shore and dismembered body parts discovered out in the woods. The notion of bear attacks was eliminated when there were no claw marks found on these bodies, fueling the legends of the man-beast stalking the area. The village, the cannery, and the mine all began to crumble as people found better and safer prospects elsewhere. By 1950, the post office in Port Chatham closed, and what was once a thriving small community became a ghost town.

Following abandonment, stories of Hairy Man sightings still emanated from Port Chatham as hunters and brave explorers continued to venture into the area around the old town site. One man in 1968 was in the area hunting goats and claimed he was chased out of the area by the creature. Three other hunters in 1973 took shelter in the ruins during a storm that ravaged the area for three straight days, and they insisted that at night something with two feet lurked outside their tents.

Of course, there are a plethora of more "conventional" Sasquatch sightings throughout Alaska as well. The Last Frontier seems to almost be the first frontier for these types of cryptids as the sightings here are abundant. Reports of Sasquatch sightings go back some 120 years, and while the most famous piece of film that captured the creature was shot in northern California in 1967, the very first film that is believed to have caught a Sasquatch on camera came out of Alaska. Only a few seconds in length, the piece of footage was shot in Mountain View in 1948.

The number of yearly Sasquatch sightings in Alaska seemingly run in direct competition with the number of UFO sightings and are certainly too numerous to mention them all here. However, these sightings are continuing to get more interesting. In March 2021, large raised footprints were discovered *atop* an Alaska ice flow, walking in a manner that seemed to indicate it had two feet. The photos took social media by storm, while the Denali National Park Service claimed they were wolf prints, "created when a wolf compressed the snow under its paws and then a strong wind blew the surrounding loose snow away." To address the seeming bipedal nature of the steps the creature took, the Park stated these appear as such due to wolves having, "an efficient stride." The photos are still hotly contested, as most photos connected to Sasquatch legend and lore usually are, but if they're real they would pose to be some of the more interesting set of tracks recorded to date.

On *The Alaska Triangle* television show, the first half of the final episode of Season 1 explored some of these stories with cryptozoologist Cliff Barackman near Lake Iliamna, an area known well for sightings of strange creatures as we'll see below, and also an interesting account involving a set of large, strange footprints that walked on for some distance. These tracks, captured in 2012 alongside the Chena River near Fairbanks by local metal detector Keith Lindsey, were more of your classical depressions into the mud rather than the tracks sitting atop the ice flow in Denali National Park. However, these tracks were similar in the fact that the strides appeared bipedal in nature – something walking on two feet definitely created these. However, the strides that created these were far longer than any normal human walking gait. Lindsey compared the footprints, which looked like large human feet, to his 11-inch metal detecting coil, and the prints were at least 5 – 6 inches longer.

Did the prints belong to a Sasquatch, a Hairy Man, a bushman, or a giant? It's another one of those elusive mysteries of the Alaska Triangle.

Lake Iliamna's Loch Ness Monster

To call the creature lurking about in Lake Iliamna it's Loch Ness Monster is a little silly since Loch Ness is thousands of miles away in Scotland, but it's natural to draw comparisons. Sightings of each creature are sporadic and steeped in lore, and each are presumed to either be a dinosaur who has survived the test of time or a much larger version of a more modern-day waterborne animal.

Floatplane on the water in Alaska.

Even the nicknames of the creatures, "Illie" for Lake Iliamna's sea creature and "Nellie" for Loch Ness's, are distinctly similar.

At 77 miles long and 22 miles wide, Lake Iliamna is Alaska's largest lake and the second largest fresh water lake in the United States, and commercial reports of the sea creature have been flowing out of the area in short bursts since 1942 when Babe Alyesworth and Bill Hammersley were flying over the lake and reported seeing a large, dull, aluminum-colored fish in the water all the way from the heights of their plane. Prior to that, the stories of something lurking in the waters of the lake attacking boats and kayaks had been relegated to legends handed down by First Nations people or Russian fur traders from the 1700s. In 1963, a biologist reported spotting a 25 – 30-foot fish in the water from overhead, and in 1967 it was a missionary who spotted something massive.

Chuck Crapuchettes is most known for founding the Cook Inlet Academy in 1972, a Christian-based school that serves children preschool through high school. Prior to establishing the academy, Crapuchettes was a missionary whose work included six years teaching at a tiny school in Newhalen on Lake Iliamna, but he'd also spent time working as a big game guide, commercial pilot, and commercial fisherman. He was an honest man, a learned one as well, and an outdoorsman. So, when he reported having an experience with Illie in 1967, people listened. And he made that claim twice.

One of these sightings by Crapuchettes saw some significant action between the creature and one of Chuck's friends. Chuck was flying a float plane overhead when he saw the behemoth in the water and radioed down to the surface for others to verify the sighting. Those on the shore had a difficult time getting a visual of Illie from shore, so one of Crapuchettes' pilot friends attached stainless-steel cables with large eight-inch tuna hooks baited with caribou onto the struts of his floatplane and flew out onto the lake. He drifted the craft on the water for a short while when all of a sudden, the plane was wrenched hard and knocked the pilot off the floats where he'd been observing. The creature tore off across Lake Iliamna with the floatplane in its grasp leaving the pilot stranded in the cold water and swimming for shore. The plane was later found abandoned miles away with three of the stainless-steel cables ripped away from the struts, and the few large hooks that remained had been perfectly straightened out by tremendous force.

Other sightings of the prodigious animal permeated the area over the years, and at one point, the Anchorage Daily News offered a substantial reward for any solid proof of Illie's existence. The prize went unclaimed, however, as the creature's movements continued to be elusive.

In 2017, the stories of the Lake Iliamna creature resurfaced when several people began seeing something massive out in the waters again, but this time it wasn't just a single creature. At least six adults, two with binoculars, and several children witnessed the following near Kakhonak that was described by local resident, Gary Nielson, to radio station KDLG:

There was more than one, at least three. The first was the biggest, maybe double the size of a 32-foot gillnetter. The animal either blew like a whale, or spit water from his mouth or something. The smaller animals behind him did the same but not as dramatic. They were black or very dark gray. They surfaced like whales for maybe two to three seconds about a mile off-shore. I am at a total loss as to what they could be.

Footage captured on a cell phone camera shows that what was witnessed appears to be some sort of serpent-type creature. On a separate occasion, another short video clip from the shore of Lake Iliamna appeared to represent the same type of serpent moving through the waters, the movement of which some people relate to a possible plesiosaur, the same extinct animal the Loch Ness Monster, if it truly exists, may actually be.

The Kushtaka Otter Men

Sasquatch, Hairy Man, and giants aren't the only large, fearsome beings lurking throughout the Alaska Triangle. Another type of strange creature passed down through the Tlingit indigenous lore of southeast Alaska and is still said to be stalking the area today is the Kushtaka, or Otter Man. These half man – half otter beasts are shapeshifters standing at about six to eight feet tall with glowing eyes, needle-like teeth and log tails. Their human attributes include human-like hands and feet although their fingernails are like talons. When they speak they emit a high-pitched, three-part whistle.

At times, the Kushtaka can take on the full form of a human and blend into the surrounding tribes, using recognizable human voices to lure in potential prey. This feature has caused some people to relate the beings to the shape-shifting skinwalker legends of the American southwest, although mostly, it has caused indigenous parents to vehemently warn their children of the dangerous Kushtaka who tend to target the younger generations. Because of this, folklorists have generally dismissed these legends as a way for parents to strike fear into their children so the young ones wouldn't venture too far away from home.

Kushtaka carving from an ancient war canoe found in Sitka in 1918.

The goal of the Kushtaka is to trap souls and prevent people from reincarnating. They may appear as a human trying to lure people away into the forest, or if one is injured, they may guise themselves as a person trying to help. However, it's all a ruse until they get the person alone and attack. Some of these attacks are purely brutal in nature as they morph back into the otter creature and tear their victims apart with their talons. At other times, the creature may spare the life of its prey and turn their victim into another Kushtaka, thus trapping the soul. This supernatural transformation is very similar to what happens to victims in the wendigo legends of the Great Lake regions and central Canada in which a wendigo attack can result in the creation of another wendigo.

The thought of being turned into a Kushtaka and losing one's soul is terrifying to the Tlingit people, especially considering their reincarnation beliefs. In order to be reincarnated into a human, one must die a human and find peace in the afterlife. Therefore, if someone suffers an attack from a Kushtaka and makes it back to the village alive, a shaman will work tirelessly to restore the person to full humanity.

Resurrection of the Woolly Mammoths

Do woolly mammoths still exist? Conventionally, most woolly mammoths across Asia and North America died out and went extinct about 13,000 years ago during global climate change that shrunk their natural habitat. A handful, however, continued to persevere on the small Alaskan island of St. Paul, devoid of human life, for several more millennia. Then, approximately 5,600 years ago, the handful of mammoths on St. Paul died out because they ran out of fresh water. It's been believed that these mammoths were the absolute last of their kind on Earth, but there's been a growing suspicion that there may be a pocket or two of woolly mammoths remaining in the ultra-remote regions of the great white north.

Alaska, the last frontier, contains a whopping 57 million acres of wilderness, much of it still unexplored where any number of creatures could be wandering. Even in today's day and age we're still discovering new animals and species. In 2014, a strange new species of beaked whale washed up on shore of Alaska's St. George Island. While this may be a new species to our eyes who knows how long it's been out there waiting for us to find it. Are surviving mammoths still out there?

There seemed to be a number of sightings of mammoths in the late 1800s which found their way into newspapers across the country, many times mistaken as mastodons[14] or just simply

---

[14] Mastodons were smaller and had flatter skulls with straighter tusks while mammoths had more bulbous heads and curved tusks which sometimes even crossed each other.

interchanging the name of the two species within an article as if they were the same animal. For instance, a December 31, 1892, article out of Lawrence, Kansas, states:

> *The well authenticated fact that a living mastodon has been seen in the center of Alaska will fire Prof. Dyche's ambition like vitriol. The possession of a stuffed mammoth by the University would place it out of sight ahead of all the institutions on the continent.*

Three months later, the Winnipeg Daily Free Press out of Manitoba printed the following concerning a mammoth sighting in Alaska:

> *He described the creature as being as large as a post trader's store, with great, shining, yellowish white tusks, and a mouth large enough to swallow a man with one gulp. He further says that the animal was undoubtedly of the same species as whose bones and tusks lie all over that section of the country.*

Artist's interpretation of woolly mammoths on a snowy plain.

There are several more of these accounts from the time period recounting brief interactions with mammoths or of just tracking their prints in the snow and mud, much like today's seekers of Sasquatch. Some skeptics believe these reports were simply explorers and hunters confused by seeing trapped remains of frozen mammoths within glacial ice which can certainly happen. Scores of frozen mammoths are still found today, which is one reason why they're so fascinating – they're a prehistoric animal which we can study fairly extensively and actually visually see what one once truly looked like. These creatures are sometimes so well preserved in the ice that rumors once circulated that the annual Explorers Club dinner actually served mammoth meat as part of their exotic cuisine in 1951. This may or may not have been true, but in 1898, Reverend Sheldon Jackson of Sitka claimed he sliced off a piece of mammoth meat from one of the giant behemoths trapped in glacial ice and fed it to his dogs.

Of all the creatures presented in this chapter, this is the one we absolutely know for certain actually did exist on this Earth, and whether or not there are small pockets of them remaining in the Alaskan wilderness we may actually see them again soon. Scientists revealed in September 2021 that they're secured funding for research in resurrecting the long extinct land animal. While the DNA extracted from woolly mammoths trapped in the permafrost is, technically, too fragmented and degraded to create a straight clone, they believe they have enough to create a hybrid elephant-mammoth that, visually, looks the same, perhaps by as early as 2025. It sounds like something out of *Jurassic Park*.

Other scientists, however, are concerned about the conservation of endangered species. Love Dalén, professor of evolutionary genetics at the Centre for Palaeogenetics in Stockholm who works on mammoth evolution, remarked about the effort, "If endangered species have lost genes that are important to them ... the ability to put them back in the endangered species, that might prove really important. ... I still wonder what the bigger point would be. First of all, you're not going to get a mammoth. It's a hairy elephant with some fat deposits. ... We, of course, have very little clue about what genes make a mammoth a mammoth. We know a little, bit but we certainly don't know anywhere near enough."

Here's something else to consider. If we create genetically-engineered mammoths that are, essentially, just a hairy elephant that looks like the woolly mammoths of old, and we introduce them out into the wild, what would happen if they encounter a lost pocket of true mammoths? Would interbreeding between these two create an even different type of hybrid, one that's part-pure woolly mammoth and part human-engineered? What would something like that look like or act like? Only in Alaska.

Chapter 8

SPECTERS OF THE NORTH

Alaska is a haunted state. That may sound overly-simplistic, but it's true and quite to the point. In my experience, having lived in several different states over the years – Ohio, Massachusetts, Alaska, Maryland, Oklahoma, and Illinois (with a couple of brief tenures in Texas and Mississippi for Air Force training) – and having visited all but two as of this writing, I can fairly soundly say that all states are rather haunted, just very differently. Each locale has its own history, its own prominent place in time which continues to echo forth today. The ghosts and hauntings permeating throughout the Alaska Triangle have their own unique personality that give experiencers of this phenomena a very distinct flavor of hauntings.

Again, as with the other chapters in this book, there is far too much area to cover here to draw out for the reader all the haunted locales throughout the state, and we've discussed a few already, such as the victims of the *Princess Sophia* tragedy haunting businesses in Juneau or the shadow entities in the basement of the Alaskan Command building on Elmendorf Air Force Base. Instead, let me try to paint the picture of Alaskan hauntings with a much broader stroke.

Paranormal investigators often talk about how spirits need energy to manifest, so much so to the point that many of these investigators will include an EMF (electromagnetic field) pump in their arsenal of equipment in order to create a stronger field of energy within the environment from which the spirits presumed to be at the location can use to manifest. Those involved in the field on a much more spiritual level often cite the composition of the soul or internal spirit within all of us, that energy that can't be unmade. The prevailing hypothesis is that energy can only be transformed, so when we lose the physical body at death, the energy within us continues on, and depending on your belief system, can go on to do a variety of different things either here on Earth, on some other world, or within some other dimension. So, what happens with that energy in a much more volatile and energetic place like Alaska?

Many paranormal investigators love working either during or just after a thunderstorm. The ionization of the atmosphere from the lightning seems to energize the location, and hauntings tend to become more active. Years ago, a small group of us were investigating the ruins of the Great White House on the old 101 Ranch near Ponca City, Oklahoma, and were finding absolutely no activity. After a while, we decided to take a break and grab a bite to eat, during which time a thunderstorm rolled through. When we returned to investigate the ruins, our meters were off the charts, balls of light were dancing amongst the tree tops, and the beating of Native American drums were heard echoing from the tree line along the creek. It was an amazing evening which had become charged after the storm.

An investigation that was even more amazing which also involved a storm was at the Mineral Springs Hotel in Alton, Illinois. Not long after lightning danced across a dark purple sky over the Mississippi River, five of us witnessed the apparition of a

The Historic Anchorage Hotel in 2019.

little girl morph out of rolling black smoke on the top floor of the hotel. So, if we're experiencing these sorts of things after just a handful of lightning storms, how much more so do those who live within the highly energetic confines of the Alaska Triangle experience some sort of significant haunting? Is the type of energy dynamically affecting these hauntings magnetic, seismic, solar, purely spiritual, or some combination of all three?

Aside from the First Nations peoples who have lived in the region for millennia, Alaska is a rather transient state between its military presence, fishing and oil industries, gold rushes, and now its booming tourism. People come and go in Alaska – a lot. Therefore, although it has a rather sparse local population, the state actually has had quite a bevy of hotels. Over time, these hotels develop their own history, personality, and legends, including numerous haunted tales.

I previously mentioned the Historic Anchorage Hotel in the

chapter on shadow entities, but the hotel has more paranormal activity occurring at it than just the shadowy silhouette of a woman. The hotel is a survivor of the 1964 Great Alaskan Earthquake. While so many other buildings collapsed and streets were upended, the hotel stood its ground, essentially making it one of the oldest buildings in downtown Anchorage. How much of that energy did it absorb into its structure?

The most mysterious ghost tale of the Historic Anchorage Hotel may be that of Police Chief John "Black Jack" Sturgus who didn't actually die within the hotel but just outside of it. On February 20, 1921, Sturgus was found dead just a few steps away from the hotel, shot in the back from his own gun. He was the city's first Chief of Police, and his murder is still unsolved to this day. His ghost periodically returns to the scene of the crime, perhaps searching for clues or just lamenting his untimely demise. Other spirits within the building include a woman who hung herself after her fiancé left her for a gold rush, a happy little boy, and an insane old woman. While their stories are not as well-known as the Sturgus story, the hotel keeps a log book for all ghost sightings. This is not the only haunted hotel in downtown Anchorage, however.

Built just after the aforementioned 1964 quake, the massive 18-story Captain Cook Hotel might not have a lengthy history, but it does have haunts of its own, including the classic woman in white. In 1972, a young woman took her life in the restroom and ever since then guests have reported an assortment of strange activity in that part of the hotel. These reports include lights flickering on and off, stall doors flying open, and sink faucets turning themselves on. When maintenance comes in to fix whatever issue may be occurring, they report nothing wrong in the room, so sometimes management will venture in and ask the ghost girl to stop making all the commotion. On occasion, the girl will actually appear to guests as a young woman in her 20s dressed in white with a

The Alaskan Hotel in 2009. Photograph: Wknight94
https://commons.wikimedia.org/w/index.php?curid=8632615

strained look on her face.

Probably the most famous haunted hotel in Alaska is that of the Alaskan Hotel in the state's capital of Juneau which has been featured on a number of television shows, including *The Alaska Triangle*. The hotel opened in 1913, so it was in operation in Juneau during the *Princess Sophia* tragedy, but that's not what it's known for. On May 19, 2007, a young sailor from aboard the *USS Bunker Hill* and in town for the evening requested to stay in the hotel's Room 315 because it was reportedly haunted, and the staff happily obliged. They had no idea the horror that was about to occur.

According to 22-year-old Americorps volunteer Jill Weitz who was staying in the room below, "I remember hearing yelling but kind of just assumed that it was coming from the bar downstairs. We hear glass shatter from above and within moments our window within our hotel room just shatters."

Juneau police officer Chris Gifford was on the scene answering a disturbance call put in on the room and had been knocking on the door of Room 315 when the glass started shattering. "We're still knocking on the door and a guy comes up and kind of whispers to me, 'Hey I think your guy just jumped out the window,'" Gifford later recalled.

Gifford and his team broke down the door and were shocked at what they saw. The walls were dripping in blood and the sailor who had rented the room was nowhere to be found within it. He had jumped out the window. With the building next door just a few feet away from the Alaskan Hotel, the young man, essentially, bounced between the buildings on the way down, smashing out windows as he plummeted. Amazingly, the sailor survived the fall and walked out to the street a bloody mess, but alive. He was medivaced to a nearby hospital and, amazingly, fully recovered from the ordeal.

So, is the Alaskan Hotel truly haunted?

During the disturbance of Room 315 prior to the sailor's jump out the window, multiple voices were heard yelling at each other within the room although the young man was the only one inside it. Was someone or something else in the room with him?

On the floor below is Room 219 where during the gold rush era a young woman named Alice lived in the room with her boyfriend. He left her there to go find gold, but when he didn't return and Alice ran out of money she started working in the hotel's bordello. During the Alaskan Hotel's early days, the building played host to a raucous crowd as sordid sorts drifted through the area in search of fortune, few finding it, and many drinking their misfortunes away. It was the classic wild west in the great white north. The boyfriend eventually returned, however, and when he discovered that Alice had turned to prostitution, he became enraged and murdered her. Her confused and much maligned spirit is said to still haunt the room and possibly other parts of the hotel today.

Additionally, the basement of the Alaskan is said to have had a resident poltergeist ever since a man drowned in a hot tub there. This angry spirit generally targets women when they venture downstairs.

We see very similar history and hauntings play out at the Red Onion Saloon in Skagway, another one of those ports en route to the Klondike. Opening in 1898, this establishment served as a saloon, brothel, and dance hall to the rowdy gold miners trekking their way through the area.

Red Onion Saloon in 1933. Photograph:
Historic American Buildings Survey

There are two prominent spirits here. One is Lydia, a former working girl whose footsteps are commonly heard throughout the second floor, but her full-bodied apparition has been seen as well, including at least one appearance in which she was observed hanging from the ceiling in a noose. Her story is a sad one as she, like so many others, took up prostitution in the bordello when her husband hadn't returned from the gold mines. (Are you starting to see a common theme here?) Her apparition has been witnessed with a scar on her cheek, possibly the mark of a prostitute with syphilis, basically ending her career. With her husband gone and no way to make a living if that's truly why she had the scar, Lydia took her own life.

Another entity witnessed at the Red Onion is more oppressive in nature and, at times, is seen as dark and shadowy. In what seemed like a playback of events one evening, a bartender witnessed a scene full of apparitions appear in the bar in which a large, boorish man was manhandling several of the working women. Suddenly, one of the women, tired of his harsh treatment, stabbed the man with a knife. It's believed by some that this man was a bouncer at the saloon and is also the spirit that sometimes appears as the dark, oppressive entity elsewhere in the saloon building.

This playback of events as described above is known to paranormal investigators as a *residual haunt*. Sometimes seen as an entire event played out like the bar scene at the Red Onion Saloon or sometimes as just a solitary apparition walking silent and sentinel, there is no interaction with the living during these viewings. The experience is simply as if someone hit the "Play" button on a television remote to watch a movie. How this phenomenon may actually work is through what some call *stone tape theory*, the idea that a recording of a highly energetic event can become trapped in nearby stone or metal in ways similar to how data is recorded to magnetic tape in order to be accessed again at a later date. The current term is derived from the 1972 BBC Christmas ghost story production called *The Stone Tape*, but its roots may go back to the late Nineteenth Century when Edmund Gurney and Eleanor Sidgwick of the Society for Psychical Research presented the idea that certain buildings and construction materials are capable of storing records of the past.

What exactly the catalyst is for the playback is unknown – we don't have television remotes for the paranormal – but it's believed environmental factors may play a part in this. Given the general volatility and strange magnetic properties of the Alaska Triangle, it stands to reason that these types of playbacks could certainly be occurring more often in that region of the world than elsewhere.

This type of theory regarding trapped energy becoming captured in building material as a recording is also related to *psychometry*, the ability to determine associations and origins of an object of unknown history by simply making physical contact with that object. Proposed in 1842 by Joseph Rodes Buchanan, the idea is that objects have their own energy fields that are able to transfer knowledge and information. The concept has been criticized by mainstream science, but during my own very first paranormal investigation I witnessed such a thing with my own eyes.

Back during the spring of 1989 when I was still in high school, my friend David and I were at our friend Loree's house just hanging out in her living room. At one point during the conversation Loree told us she believed her house was haunted. She had been living in an older, historic home in the downtown area of our small town, and she proceeded to tell us about the creepy family cemetery in the backyard and some of the strange occurrences within the house. Her primary concern was with the one wall in her bedroom upstairs – she couldn't tack anything up on it. No matter what she did, within an hour, a day, or a week, whatever poster or object she tried placing on the wall would always fall down. Ever the adventurous souls, David and I decided we were going to check this out. We were upstairs in Loree's bedroom taking a look at the wall as she continued to tell us more stories when David promptly put his hand flat on the wall. Suddenly, my friend turned bright red and started sweating profusely. Having never seen anything like this before, I was absolutely amazed. As I stood there, awestruck, David proceeded to go wall-to-wall throughout the house trying to find more "hot spots."

My friend absolutely felt an energy within that wall emanating forth, and I could see with my own eyes how it physically affected him. Now, this event occurred in just a small town in Ohio. While

Ohio is certainly a fairly haunted state with its own distinct energy, how much more so would David have felt this kind of energy pouring forth in a dynamically more energetic area of the world like Alaska?

We also talked earlier about time slips in Chapter 5, and time slips could certainly be occurring when we see some of these spectral apparitions play out. If all moments in time are happening together concurrently, perhaps it's just a matter of accessing that wavelength or frequency in order to view the moment, and that scene, like the one of the bouncer with the working ladies, comes off looking like an apparition to our eyes.

Journalist John Keel breaks this down rather nicely in his 1971 book, *Our Haunted Planet*:

Electrical energy is also discussed at great length in terms of vibrations, and this material can be easily translated into contemporary terms of wave lengths and frequencies. Ancient man knew that smashing the atom yields pure energy. He knew that human eyes could only see a tiny portion of the electromagnetic spectrum (visible light), and he believed that other worlds or realities existed beyond the limitations of his sight.

Specter, the ancient word for ghostly apparition, sprang from spectrum. *Early peoples observed that these objects or entities were able to reflect or cast off light wavelengths from the entire visible spectrum from violet at one end to red at the other. They knew they were seeing transmogrifications of electrical energy.*

The era we've primarily been discussing, the late-Nineteenth to early-Twentieth Century, seems to be an extraordinarily stained time in Alaskan history as we've seen on a number of occasions throughout this book. How many people were lost on shipwrecks or were last seen trudging their way through the harsh climate in search of some fortune never to be seen again, we'll never know for sure. How many women had to turn to prostitution to survive only to meet some unfortunate, grisly end? Even when the people of the time congregated on land in the relative safety of others, strange and bizarre things continued to happen.

For instance, there hasn't been a lode of copper hauled out of the Kennecott Copper mines in the Wrangell mountains since the 1930s, but the old railroad line that serviced it, the Copper River and Northwestern Railway, continues to deliver supernatural stories to this day. This 200-mile stretch of track from Kennicott Glacier to Cordova on Prince William Sound was a constant work in progress as the glacier shifted and tracks had to be moved in accordance. With 129 bridges traversing swirling rivers, tracks clinging to sheer walls of rock, and workers digging themselves out from snow and the occasional avalanche, it's a wonder the line was ever completed. The total number of lives lost during

Camp of workers during construction of the Copper River and Northwestern Railway in 1909. Photograph: Eric Hegg

construction is unknown, and plenty of additional lives were lost while the area was actively being mined over 30 years.

When the mines finally dried up and the railroad stopped running, the communities along the line turned into ghost towns virtually overnight. In time, the National Park Service salvaged the area and turned a region of mostly abandoned buildings into a small tourist attraction as a park and making a road out of the old railroad line east into the mountains from Chitina. It is along this stretch known as McCarthy Road and the Kennecott historical landmark off of it in which several people have reported disappearing headstones along the path heading into the park. On their way up the path, these people could distinctly see the stones standing prominent and paralleling the old copper railroad. On their way back down, however, the headstones had completely disappeared.

Construction workers for a government housing development in the late 1990s also witnessed the vanishing headstones, but they experienced other strange things as well. They claimed to have heard screams of long-deceased miners and tools all around the construction site suddenly went missing, including ones straight from the tool belts they'd been wearing. In the forest next to the old tracks, several people have also seen full-bodied apparitions walking about. Are these apparitions shadows of the past, or are these specters other moments in time coming into focus for a brief instant when we catch the frequency just right? Could some even be *intelligent haunts*, spirits whose consciousnesses are present in the very moment as if they're still living and able to interact with witnesses in real time?

This is why investigators explore the paranormal.

Chapter 9

GOVERNMENT COVER-UPS AND CONSPIRACIES

Since I spent six years in the United States Air Force, three in Alaska and three at Ft. George G. Meade in Maryland (the home of the National Security Agency), I, invariably, get asked if I know any juicy government secrets. This is especially true of my time at NSA, which we're certainly not covering in this book and didn't occur in Alaska anyway. The closest I got to NSA in Alaska was passing their office next to ours on a daily basis in the basement of the Alaskan Command building. There was an attractive brunette who worked the front reception area who I would often say, "Hi," to in passing, but that's about all that amounted to my interaction with the NSA up north.

People who follow my work need to keep in mind that I was a young airman just out of high school, so I wasn't privy to loads of government secrets even though I had a Top Secret security clearance. Top Secret clearances are compartmentalized and come with special letter assignments that designate which compartments you can gain access to if you have a *need to know*. So, while I may have had a TS/SSBI clearance, I could only enter those areas that required that access if I had a need to be there for some particular reason. My need mostly involved fixing someone's computer in that area, installing software, handling a network issue, etc. I did see a handful of things along the way, *mostly* at NSA on Ft. Meade, of course, and I was not specifically involved in any cover-ups in Alaska. However, there are several that are rumored to have occurred there.

Boggs and Begich (Brown and Jonz) Revisisted

We've already discussed the disappearance of the airplane carrying House Majority Leader Hale Boggs and Congressman Nick Begich in 1972. There are many who have believed this tragedy to have been the work of political enemies since Boggs had a falling out with several high-powered politicians after he dissented from the findings of the Warren Commission which supported the single bullet theory in the

Hale Boggs

assassination of President John F. Kennedy. Boggs didn't just simply disagree with the thesis that Lee Harvey Oswald was the lone gunman in the murder. He was so adamant about it that, according to political lawyer Bernard Fensterwald who worked on the Watergate case, Boggs once said to an aide, "[FBI Director J. Edgar] Hoover lied his eyes out to the Commission – on Oswald, on Ruby, on their friends, the bullets, the gun, you name it."

In the 1979 spy novel *The Matarese Circle*, author Robert Ludlum included a plot point in which Boggs had been killed in

Nick Begich

order to stop his investigation into the JFK assassination. Published just seven years after the tragedy, this added fuel to the growing conspiracy theory that the Boggs-Begich disappearance was no fluke accident. Some suggest if there was a conspiracy against Boggs it wasn't about the Warren Commission but about the growing Watergate scandal against President Richard Nixon.

Two decades later following a Freedom of Information Act request of the investigation documents, the Washington D.C. newspaper *Roll Call* reported on August 3, 1992:

> *The day after an airplane carrying House Majority Leader Hale Boggs (D-La) and Rep. Nick Begich (D-Alaska) vanished in Alaska 20 years ago, the US Coast Guard received a mysterious report that a radio call from the downed plane had been picked up and that two of the plane's four passengers were still alive.*
>
> *The story of the report, which has never before been revealed, is contained in FBI documents obtained last week by Roll Call under a Freedom of Information Act request. The source of the report, whose identity was censored, was judged credible, but there is evidence that the Coast Guard may not have followed up the report quickly, if at all.*

Although the report reinvigorated a perplexed public, not to mention the families wanting answers, an investigation for the missing plane wasn't renewed. Officials at the time stated that the area had been searched many times over for other crashes over the years, and nothing had ever turned up regarding the Cessna 310 carrying Boggs and Begich.

Twenty-six years later in 2018, John Greenewald of The Black Vault[15], the largest privately run online repository of declassified government documents in the world, submitted his own Freedom of Information Act request on the case and received back a heavily redacted 398-page document[16] which included some interesting additional information. Within the documentation are interviews with a person-of-interest who provided information about his involvement in several homicides in Alaska and also divulged information about the Boggs – Begich disappearance. Several documents repeat the same conversation, but here's the redacted transcript from FBI correspondence to the Department of Justice regarding the matter dated October 19,1995:

... also known as

...

... also known as

...

THOMAS HALE BOGGS, also known as
Hale Boggs – VICTIM (DECEASED);
NICHOLAS JOSEPH BEGICH, also known as
Nick Begich – VICTIM (DECEASED);
RUSSELL L. BROWN – VICTIM (DECEASED);
DON E. JONZ – VICTIM (DECEASED);
INTERSTATE TRANSPORTATION IN AID OF RACKETEERING – MURDER FOR HIRE
(NON-ORGANIZED CRIME)

The Anchorage Office of the Federal Bureau of Investigation (FBI) received information from the Alaska State Troopers (AST) and the Anchorage Police Department (APD) that one ... expressed a desire to clear up several unsolved homicides in the State of Alaska ... provided information concerning his involvement

---

[15] https://www.theblackvault.com/

[16] https://documents.theblackvault.com/documents/fbifiles/politicians/thomasboggs-fbi1.pdf

and knowledge of three homicides in Alaska in ... to AST and APD investigators.

Prior to concluding the interview ... discussed his possible involvement in suspicious activities that may have contributed to aircraft disappearance on October 16, 1972, of a Cessna 310 which carried U.S. House Majority Leader Thomas Hale Boggs and U.S. Representative Nicholas Joseph Begich.

In summary ... stated that he met ... in Tucson, Arizona, in the company of ... and ... in September, 1972, ... stated that he transported a suitcase to Anchorage, Alaska, at the request of ... delivered the locked suitcase to one ... at the Anchorage International Airport, Anchorage, Alaska. ... was in the company of one ... stated that he became good friends with ... and on a fishing trip was told that the suitcase that he had transported in 1972, contained "high tech explosives." ... then stated that the suitcase was subsequently put on the aircraft that carried Boggs and Begich to Juneau, Alaska. Further ... stated that ... admitted to him that ... .

A review of the various documents/records to include ... interviews, wrongful deaths suits, newspaper articles and FBI files indicated that ... allegations appear to be unfounded. The weather was extremely poor on the morning of the flight. The largest search in the history of the State of Alaska was conducted by numerous local, state and federal agencies. No plane wreckage, bodies or crime scene were discovered by authorities.

Records revealed that there were extensive investigation and court hearings on this matter in the 1970s and 1980s. There is no evidence of a violation of the law surrounding the disappearance of the Boggs/Begich aircraft disappearance. On September 13, 1995, Assistant U.S. Attorney ... declined prosecution.

Apparently, this is as far as this aspect of the investigation into the missing Cessna 310 went, although conspiracy theorists have long suspected some sort of sordid foul play was involved with the disappearance. The perspective of those who don't believe there was any mischief involved is understandable. If there really had been a bomb and explosion, wouldn't remnants of the plane be found scattered all throughout Portage Pass? Then again, if there's some sort of cover-up involved, would the authorities involved really divulge information about scattered pieces of plane wreckage or would that have been swept under the carpet?

Interestingly, the cache of documents released to Black Vault also included a pile of paperwork regarding a complaint Boggs had filed about the National Broadcasting Company (NBC) planting an unauthorized listening device in the Democratic Platforms Committee hearing room at the Sheraton-Blackstone Hotel in Chicago in 1968.

The Warren Commission... Watergate... unauthorized bugging of a meeting... You make the call.

(An interesting note – and I am, by no means, making any sort of insinuation – Nick Begich, who was expected to win, did actually win his election against Don Young weeks following his disappearance. However, with Begich declared deceased, a special election was held in which Young won, and Young has, as of this writing, held the seat ever since. That's 25 consecutive terms as the Republican Party's longest-serving member of the House of Representatives in history.)

HAARP

As a whole, HAARP, the High-frequency Active Auroral Research Program has been screaming, "Conspiracy!" for decades. On the surface, it's supposed to be an antenna system that's meant to study the activity of the ionosphere. Outside of that ... well, the world has seen the likes of Venezuela leader Hugo Chavez accuse the program of much more malicious means. In 2010, he insisted the program set off the Haitian earthquake that year.

HAARP was established in 1993 as joint program between the U.S. Air Force, U.S. Navy, the University of Alaska Fairbanks, and the Defense Advanced Research Projects Agency (DARPA). After 21 years of operation, the Air Force announced in 2014 it

The controversial HAARP in 2010.

was shutting down HAARP, but less than a year later it found new life when the operation was transferred over to the University of Alaska Fairbanks who still controls it as of today. But what is it that makes this device so controversial that some people, like former governor of Minnesota Jesse Ventura, claim it's a mind-control device while others claim the array can control the weather?

The HAARP site is massive. Spread out over 30 acres in Gakona, it contains 180 phased array antennae, each one standing an impressive 72 feet tall. The area of the sky it's supposed to be studying, the ionosphere, is equally impressive as it stretches from 30 miles above the Earth's surface to 600 miles up. This is where solar flares meet head-on collisions with the Earth's magnetic shield, where auroras are created, and it makes sense to house this type of device in Alaska where that protection is thinnest. In fact, while scientists at HAARP insist the antenna array can't change the weather, the device did create the first artificial aurora in 2005.

Todd Peterson of the Air Force Research Laboratory told *LiveScience* at that time, "The radio waves travel up to the ionosphere, where they excite the electrons in the plasma. These electrons then collide with atmospheric gasses, which then give off light, as in a neon tube."

What concerned most people with this statement is the idea that HAARP was used to "excite the electrons" and directly affect conditions in the Earth's atmosphere. This has led to a bevy of accusations of weather events HAARP is said to have been a direct cause of, including the 2011 earthquake and tsunami in Japan, the 2013 tornado in Moore, Oklahoma, a 2006 landslide in the Philippines, and the aforementioned earthquake in Haiti, among many others. Chavez's accusation about the earthquake stemmed from a French satellite named DEMETER (Detection of Electro-Magnetic Emissions Transmitted from Earthquake Regions) detecting ultra-low frequency radio waves over Haiti within a month before the earthquake hit. There is no way to substantiate that these waves came from HAARP, but Michael Athanasiou at the Technical University of Serres in Greece stated, "The results reveal a significant increase of the energy of ULF waves, up to 360%, for a period of one month before the main earthquake compared with the energy of the background."

Co-author of the 1995 book *Angels Don't Play This HAARP*, Dr. Nick Begich, son of the missing congressman, described HAARP as, "A super-powerful radiowave-beaming technology that lifts areas of the ionosphere by focusing a beam and heating those areas. Electromagnetic waves then bounce back onto earth and penetrate everything — living and dead."

So, if these electromagnetic waves penetrate *everything*, including the Earth's crust, then how might these waves interact with and effect the telluric currents that are already running within the ground? Is, perhaps, another reason HAARP is positioned in Alaska because of the volatility in the land and an opportunity to harness additional power from the Alaska Triangle?

Dr. Begich, whose health science background includes a strong interest in electrophysiology, the effect of electromagnetic fields on the human body, is also an advocate of the HAARP mind control theory, postulating this idea in his book as well as in the 2018 documentary *Mind Control: HAARP & The Future of Technology*, describing how Alaska was the perfect location for this type of technology,

The ideal place for this in the United States happened to be the north slope of Alaska where you have huge supplies of natural gas, and you also have close proximity to the magnetic fields that intersect the Earth.

Very low frequency energy can be pumped up into the ionosphere and when it arrives there it captures some of the localized energy and amplifies the signal by 1000 times. Now, that's huge and this is something that Stanford discovered and something that fits right in to the profile on HAARP, because here you have this primer, this small bit of energy you can manipulate, and then you use the Earth itself as the key to your weapon system.

Anyone who's followed the development of weapons systems we are intending to move further and further away from bombs and bullets and ordinance, and more into things that affect us on a much more profound level using electromagnetic fields as a primary weapon of the future.

Eventually, [the research] all flows back to one place, or two places, Central Intelligence, NSA, these are areas that they're very interested in as well as DARPA which then decides how it's farmed out in terms of applied technology.

Dr. Begich's concerns lie in the fact that HAARP is the largest producer of extremely low frequency signals in the world which, while it can perform surface scans of large areas of land, ELF signals are also biologically active in human beings. This means that ELF signals can directly interact with a human being and create changes within us. This essentially creates a frequency following response which is a prime factor in brain entrainment where the brain recognizes an external signal and begins to lock on to it and mirror it. Dr. Begich continues in *Mind Control*:

> *These ranges can be affected through what's called brain entrainment which is an external signal, or what's called frequency following response, where the brain will recognize certain signals in a very similar way to dialing through a radio to pick up the radio signal. You get a nice clear signal when you have harmony between transmitter and receiver, or you have resonance between the receiver and the transmitter. The same is true with the human body.*
>
> *This is what HAARP does on a hemispeheric scale, because what happens is a high frequency signal coming off the transmitter on the ground hits an area called the ionosphere which is about 30 miles above the Earth's surface, and then what it does is they pulse that high frequency signal. So, it's like a hammer hitting the head of a nail, and every time it hits the ionosphere vibrates like a bell sending back a signal to the Earth in an extremely low frequency range. This would alter behavior over a pretty wide and large geographic area.*

Is the government using HAARP as a mind control device as we speak? Are they truly able to control the weather just like they created an artificial aurora in the sky? It's hard to definitively say they're actively doing these things, but the technology is in place in Alaska, and they've been studying and experimenting for decades.

This technology HAARP has been using in Gakona is also now antiquated. Over the years, as with other technologies we've developed, devices have gotten smaller yet much more powerful. They likely no longer need 30 acres of land to achieve the same results. Are there smaller, perhaps Top Secret installations utilizing HAARP-based technology now much more advanced, generations ahead of where they had started back in 1993?

Chapter 10

OTHER CONNECTIONS

At initial glance, Alaska seems to be some sort of rogue northern world, isolated and frozen at the top of the planet. Its nearest neighbors who experience the same arctic climate include Canada and Russia, but Alaska has connections to other parts of the world as well, as far away as you could get, in fact. How might Alaska be connected to, say … Antarctica?

It's not as crazy of a notion as it sounds. Alaska and Antarctica both share extremely cold climates, they both rest at the geographical top or bottom of the world, and they have both been home to the same magnetic poles. Yes, at certain points within our planet's history, if you were to look at a compass pointing north it would actually have been pointing toward what we currently call the South Pole, today's home to Antarctica.

As of this writing, magnetic North has wandered about a 685-mile trek of northern Canada over the past 150 years and, in recent decades, has sped up to about 25 miles per year toward the northwest (closer to Alaska), which some believe indicate a polar flip is in the near future. According to an analysis in the journal *Science*, a well-preserved ancient tree has helped scientists deduced the last polar flip occurred about 42,000 years ago. The flip was short-lived, however. According to evolutionary biologist Alan Cooper with Blue Sky Genetics and the South Australian Museum, "Even though it was short, the North Pole did wander across North America, right out towards New York, actually, and then back again to Oregon." He continued to describe that it, "then zoomed down through the Pacific really fast to Antarctica and hung out there for about 400 years and then shot back up through the Indian Ocean to the North Pole again."

Four hundred years is just a blip on the history of Earth, but when we talk about human history, that's a pretty significant chuck of change. Four hundred years ago in the 1620s, the *Mayflower* had just landed at Plymouth Rock, the *First Folio* of William Shakespeare was published (feel free to debate who actually wrote it), and King Louis XIII began the first construction of the Palace of Versailles as a hunting lodge. In the animal kingdom, the last of the aurochs died in 1627 in the Jaktorow Forest in Poland. A lot has happened since that time, and there's a lot humanity could have accomplished in four centuries some 42,000 years ago, but that's beyond the scope of this book.

It's hard to say what Antarctica may have experienced during its 400 years as the North Pole since so much evidence is trapped under the ice, but it may have been quite a hotter experience. During the time of the pole shift, the Earth's protective magnetic shield would have been in flux, down to as much as 6% of its current state, causing dramatic climate change. The solar wind from the sun would have pounded the earth with radiation and likely causing the extinction of many species. The air would have been more ionized – a fantastic conductor of electricity – creating far more electrical storms and aurora sightings all over the Earth.

According to Professor Cooper, "Early humans around the world would have seen amazing auroras, shimmering veils, and sheets across the sky. It must have seemed like the end of days."

Was every night a world-wide light show 40,000 years ago?

Is this, perhaps, why we're discovering so many cave drawings around the world from that timeframe? Had humans taken shelter there to protect themselves from the scorching sun and wild electrical storms? Could Antarctica have been more habitable during this time? Hold that thought for a moment. We'll come back to that soon.

I'm not going to launch into a full discussion on Antarctica in this book – the material on our southernmost continent could take up its own entire volume, but we ought to look at some of its properties and discuss whether or not the same could be said of Alaska. To do so, we need look no further than Antarctica's ANITA project for our first taste of something extraordinary occurring near the South Pole.

The ANITA (Antarctic Impulsive Transient Antenna) is a stratospheric balloon-based experiment which points a radio antenna back at Earth to try to detect radio waves that are emitted by high-energy neutrinos if they happen to strike an atom in the ice. Back in 2016, ANITA detected evidence of high-energy neutrinos coming up out of the Earth's surface without a source. The findings prompted the publication of a *New Scientist* article which stated, "Explaining the signal requires the existence of a topsy-turvy universe created in the same big bang as our own and existing in parallel with it. In this mirror world, positive is negative, left is right, and time runs backwards."

This controversial statement took the internet by storm as other publications followed up by declaring there had been the discovery of a parallel universe running in reverse time. The mainstream brushed this aside, but I'm not going to enter that debate here. I will explore this concept more in-depth in my next book, *Connecting the Universe*. However, if these findings in Antarctica are true and the poles were once reversed as we discussed earlier, could those same findings with the neutrinos have been found in Alaska during the time the poles had been flipped? Could they actually be found there now?

Alaska has been nicknamed "The Last Frontier" for quite a long time, but Antarctica is equally enigmatic. There are answers to mysteries buried miles under the ice which scientists and explorers are dying to discover. Will they share it with us when they find it? Like Alaska, there are rumors in Antarctica of UFO sightings dating back, possibly, as far as Admiral Richard Byrd during Operation Highjump (1946 – 1947) when he led a Top Secret expedition to the South Pole, inspired by, many say, Nazi documents acquired during World War II which depicted flying saucers. Byrd is said to have intercepted these UFOs during his sojourn to Antarctica and was never the same when he returned.

As UFO sightings began increasing during the late 1940s and early 1950s, Albert K. Bender founded the International Flying Saucer Bureau in 1952 but quickly disbanded it a year later when he was visited by three shadowy, hat-wearing entities who warned him off his research. He claimed these entities were part of a faction of extraterrestrials who occupied Antarctica and were harvesting its water for resources until they had enough of the material they needed to leave in the early 1960s. Is what's attractive in Antarctica the same as what's attractive in Alaska, causing all the recent UFO sightings there?

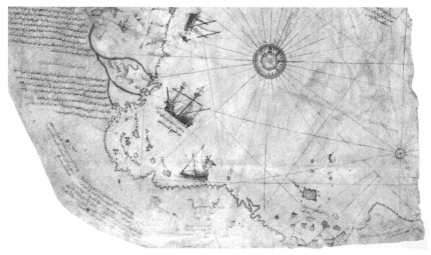

The bottom portion of the 1513 Piri Reis map depicting the tip of South America and part of the coastline of Antarctica. What has survived of the map, which includes South and Central American coastlines and a part of Africa's west coast, is only a third of the original work. Reis created this based on several historic maps lost to time, including a map that was said to have been created by Christopher Columbus.

What's so attractive to our heavy military and scientific presence at the South Pole, so secretive that each individual organization has no idea what the other ones are doing? Not only was there a pole shift, but the Antarctica island wasn't once where it currently rests. The land was once further north in a warmer climate. A handful of ancient maps, such as the 1513 Piri Reis map, accurately depicts the continent of Antarctica (curiously, long before its "discovery" in 1820) although in a slightly different location. Land masses, naturally, move about via continental drift and, perhaps, via Earth crust displacement, as theorized by Charles Hapgood. Antarctica, it seems, may have drifted or been displaced to where it now sits more recently than other areas of the world, which is not unheard of as different tectonic plates around the globe move at varying speeds. (In 2016, for example, *National Geographic* published an article boasting "Australia Is Drifting So Fast GPS Can't Keep Up.")

So, if this is true, and Antarctica was much more accessible to the world population than it is now, who would have settled this continent that now rests at the South Pole? There's a fantastic maritime race of legend that could have colonized that stretch of land, a race legendary for its amazing concentric city but also one which spread its wings across the seas. It's been widely believed that remnants of Atlantis can be found in many parts of the world, survivors who forged new civilizations after the collapse of their own. Many of those surviving civilizations, such as Egypt, still mystify us as to how they built the amazing structures we see today, structures we can't currently build or have just now developed the technology to do so. How did they perform these miraculous feats? How did they machine their works during a time in history that the conventional mainstream tells us these peoples were only using copper, something that could never have built and carved the pyramids or so many of the magnificent granite sculptures that have stood the test of time?

If the Egyptians are the descendants of the Atlanteans and there are Atlantean remains under the ice in Antarctica, then is the technology the Egyptians used to build their structures buried under the ice at the South Pole as well? What if that technology includes some sort of anti-gravity device these ancient peoples employed to build their magnificent wonders, passed down by their Atlantean forebearers? Wouldn't discovering that be worth the substantial and costly effort that's been launched in Antarctica? Is that what the Nazi's were searching for in the frozen wasteland during World War II?

Again, the depth of this discussion is beyond the scope of this book, but I wanted to introduce it here since it's another area of research I've started exploring and felt the premise of it needed to be published at this point. Plus ... there are those connections back to Alaska.

If the Atlanteans were aware of and settled Antarctica, perhaps even using some of its magnetic properties for use in stargate technology or accessing a parallel dimension running in reverse like some have concluded with the ANITA project results, did they also know about and visit Alaska if it once — and perhaps still does — have the same magnetic properties. Could there be remnants of ancient civilizations buried deep under Alaska as well, long since forgotten?

There are stories of a pyramid buried underground near Mt. Denali (formerly Mt. McKinley) in Alaska that's twice the size of the Great Pyramid of Giza in Egypt. Nicknamed "The Black Pyramid" or "The Dark Pyramid" due to the black stone it's supposed to be constructed with, this structure is said to have been discovered by geologists who were performing seismic studies of the Earth's crust following a nuclear detonation in China. Shockwaves spread out over 4,000 miles from the epicenter, and from those waves, they were able to determine a massive structure, pyramidal in shape, was contained within the mountain range.

It's a controversial subject since the story is reportedly only to have ever aired once on Anchorage's Channel 13 with no follow up, and it never aired on other local affiliate networks. A visit to the television station by a curious, young counter-intelligence operative on Ft. Richardson at that time, Doug Mutschler, was thwarted when he was told the station had no record of the segment they'd aired. Just before Mutschler left the building, a junior staff member pulled him aside and told him some other men had come by the station just after the segment aired and confiscated the tapes.

A smattering of people have come forward over the years to reveal some tidbits of information related to this mysterious pyramid, but concrete information about it seems rather elusive.

The pyramid is believed by some to have been some sort of ancient power plant used to power the entire area, including parts of Canada. Others believe the pyramid is used to help power UFOs traveling through the area. Aerial surveys of the area do reveal evidence of human activity, including a squared off clearing, remnants of an old road, and the distinct rectangular strip of a runway. Whether or not those signs of human activity are directly related to the Dark Pyramid is unknown. More detailed information can be found on Linda Moulton Howe's *Earth Files* web archive at https://www.earthfiles.com/.

The idea of this Black Pyramid or Dark Pyramid being some sort of power plant seems to correlate with what author, researcher, and machinist Christopher Dunn has postulated about the Great Pyramid of Giza, that it's the remnant of what had once been a giant power plant, an ancient machine built far longer into the ancient past than what mainstream academia is willing to admit. However, Dunn was able to venture inside the Great Pyramid several times to take measurements and formulate his theory based on a massive building that people are able to observe and tour every single day. The Black Pyramid, unfortunately, remains hidden underground in the frozen white north, and all we can do at this point is trust that the reports which have come forth are accurate.

In another ironic connection, there's a photo of a dark-colored unnamed mountain in Antarctica's Ellsworth mountain range that looks so much like a pyramid that several websites have used the photo in their articles about Alaska's Dark Pyramid (even though the Dark Pyramid is supposed to be underground). Many also believe the Antarctic mountain itself is an ancient pyramid. The photo serves almost like a visual double entendre, teasing us about two highly controversial structures in both Alaska and Antarctica shrouded in mystery and suspicion. Is there really something to these locations?

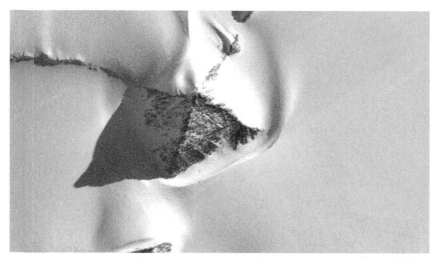

Mysterious pyramidal formation in Antarctica. Photograph: Google Earth

There does appear to be a connection between many of the pyramids and ancient sites of power around the world. For instance, the Great Pyramid of Giza is aligned with Machu Picchu, the Nazca Lines, Easter Island, Mohenjo-daro, and more. Back in Chapter 1, we discussed the significance of these alignments and why the ancients built these monumental structures along the telluric currents of the Earth. Can we put Alaska and possibly its Dark Pyramid into that mix of ancient alignments? Are there other structures in Alaska not buried under ice and rock that may point to these same alignments? Possibly.

There's also an interesting rock formation within the Alaska Triangle called the Sphinx of Ophir near Council, Alaska. Ophir is an abandoned mining town, but still serves as a checkpoint for the Iditarod Sled Dog Race. This sphinx only appears as a head with distinguishable features that includes lips, nose, eyes, and cheekbones. It also appears to be wearing some sort of headdress. It's not the classic Egyptian sphinx that comes to mind when we think of the Great Sphinx on the Giza plateau in Egypt, but it fits the basic definition with a human head and possible animalistic body. Whether this is some ancient manmade construction or just

The Sphinx of Ophir rock formation near Council, Alaska, in 1900.

an oddity of nature remains to be seen, but if it's ever determined to be a work of human hands then it's one more connection of Alaska to the ancient world.

If these structures in Alaska are what some believe them to be, then they would connect the Alaska Triangle to the Earth's most ancient history, to cultures that created the oldest civilizations on the planet. It's a concept difficult to fathom in a land that seems so remote to us today and is so sparsely populated, but the Earth didn't always appear as it does in this day and age, and the climate is continuously changing. We can't look at the ancient history of the world through the context of our own eyes. We have to refocus that lens to a planet we wouldn't recognize at all in today's modern society, whether that's during one of the ice age periods, a severe warming trend, the Earth just after The Flood, or any other era. As we previously discussed in Chapter 7, it's not out of the realm of possibility for North America to have a much older past than has previously been believed.

Graham Hancock sums it up nicely in his tome, *America Before*:

There are literally thousands of myths from every inhabited continent that speak of the existence of an advanced civilization in remote pre-history, of the lost golden age in which it flourished, and of the cataclysm that brought it to an end. A feature shared by many of them – the story of Atlantis, for example, or of Noah's flood – is the notion that human beings, by their own arrogance, cruelty, and disrespect for the earth, had somehow brought the disaster down upon their own heads and accordingly were obliged by the gods to go back to basics and learn humility again.

So, here we are, thousands of years later, on the brink of our destruction again, threatening the existence of our own modern-day civilization with chaos, violence, and disease, a cycle we can't seem to break free of as a species. We need to reexamine the timeline, look back deep into the past, and ask ourselves what really happened in our world history. How many times did civilization rise and fall over the millennia? Where did those civilizations exist? And what can we learn from them so we don't repeat the same mistakes?

FINAL THOUGHTS

On February 14, 1994, I was flying northward in a glorified tin can just over the tree tops of the Alaskan wilderness. I was on a one-day temporary assignment with a fellow airman en route to Fort Wainwright near Fairbanks. We had computers there that required maintenance, and we needed to brief the Army personnel at Wainwright on a few new procedures for accessing our communications programs. As I looked down at the landscape, which was certainly beautiful, I couldn't help but think how harsh the terrain was below us. The plane shook almost incessantly as it bounded through the air, and it was quite frigid inside the cabin even though some kind of heater was in operation. It would be 30 degrees below zero Fahrenheit in the Fairbanks area when we touched down later that morning on a runway covered in ice, but at that moment in the air I kept staring at the trees and the surrounding endless snow. What would happen to us if the plane suddenly dropped out of the sky?

I usually include a "Final Thoughts" chapter at the end of each of my nonfiction books, but that concept seems ever more pertinent with this particular volume – what were the final thoughts of the thousands of souls that have been lost within the Alaska Triangle? So many people have gone missing over the years. There's been an avalanche of heartbreak and tragedy in this one region of the world. While I've put together a couple hundred pages here that now rests in your hands telling some of these tales, it just doesn't seem right that I had to skip over so many. These were human beings who had lives waiting for them at home, who had families, who had children, and so many of them have been forgotten to time after the headlines subsided. I imagine the final thoughts for many of them were, "Will I ever see my loved ones again?"

Alaska seems like such a far away place for most people, generally relegated to a small corner of most maps of the United States, when the state is so amazingly massive. How does something so large become almost an afterthought to most Americans? Those that do acknowledge its existence are aware that Alaska is undeniably beautiful and may have even visited the great white north on one of those fantastic summer cruises. To live in Alaska is a whole other story and adventure, as treacherous as it may be. That's one of the strange dichotomies of this world we live in – so many of our most beautiful things are also some of our most dangerous.

It's almost like a whole other planet up in Alaska, and perhaps that's why it's seemingly more mysterious than most of the other triangle areas of the world. It's not easily accessible – you can't drive there without significant hours through another country – and once you're there it's unlike any other place you've ever been. Everything seems so much larger in Alaska – the mountains, the fish, the earthquakes – and that includes the mysterious forces at work there. Considering how magnetic and electromagnetic applications are now being used in agriculture for the improvement of seed germination to produce larger crops and yields, it's not surprising to find so many things larger-than-life in this highly energetic region of the world. Whoever came up with the phrase, "Go big or go home," must have had Alaska in mind. That's one of the primary reasons it's so difficult to investigate in that area – the sheer vastness of it all. It's a place where secrets can be readily hidden, whether that's from off-world, the landscape, or from the government. So, when someone goes missing how do we know if the cause had been elements of nature, or a Kushtaka, or extraterrestrials, or a portal opening and swallowing them whole, or some other strange phenomenon we haven't yet seen?

There's so much yet for us to explore in this expansive frontier, physically, spiritually, and interdimensionally. What new nuggets of knowledge await us as we continue to investigate this area of the world and uncover its mysteries? Will we find that piece of Atlantean technology that evolves us to a new state of awareness? Will we find those gateways and stargates to other systems and universes? Could we possibly harness the power of the triangle and come to understand how real time travel may actually work?

Only in Alaska.

BIBLIOGRAPHY

Aitken, Peter. "Three Volcanoes are Erupting Simultaneously on Alaskan Island Chain." *Fox News*. Accessed at: https://www.foxnews.com/science/alaska-volcanoes-erupting-simultaneously

Alaska Triangle, The. Directed by Christian Bradshaw, Wild Dream Films, 2020 – 2021.

"ALCOM Building." Accessed at: https://www.dvidshub.net/ image/3106132/alcom-building

Ancient Code. "Xelhua – The Giant Who Built Teotihuacan and the Largest Pyramid on Earth." *Ancient Code*. Accessed at: https://www.ancient-code.com/xelhua-giant-built-teotihuacan-pyramid-earth/

Aspasia Efthimiadou, Nikolaos Katsenios, Anestis Karkanis, Panayiota Papastylianou, Vassilios Triantafyllidis, Ilias Travlos, Dimitrios J. Bilalis, "Effects of Presowing Pulsed Electromagnetic Treatment of Tomato Seed on Growth, Yield, and Lycopene Content", The Scientific World Journal, vol. 2014, Article ID 369745, 6 pages, 2014.https://doi.org/10.1155/2014/369745

Baldwin, Debra. "The Missing Keepers of Eldred Rock Lighthouse: John Currie and John Silander." Lighthouse Digest. Accessed at: http://lighthousedigest.com/Digest

/StoryPage.cfm?StoryKey=4875

Barefield, Robin. "The Alaska Triangle. Is It Real?" *Medium.* Accessed at: https://medium.com/the-mystery-box/the-alaska-triangle-ce04b186ff82

Bauman, Kennon. "Dark Pyramids Under Alaska." *The Illuminerdy.* Accessed at: https://www.theilluminerdy.net/unreal-worlds/2018/2/4/dark-pyramids-under-alaska

Beauty of Birds. "Argentavis Magnificens or Giant Teratorn (Extinct)." Accessed at: https://www.beautyofbirds.com/argentavis.html

Beckstead, Doug. "Elmendorf Air Base's First Commander." Accessed at: https://www.jber.jb.mil/News/Articles/Article/292263/elmendorf-army-air-bases-first-commander/

Bird, Bob. "The Lake Iliamna Cryptid Saga." Peninsula Clarion. Accessed at: https://www.peninsulaclarion.com/life/the-lake-iliamna-cryptid-saga/

Black Vault, The. "Boggs, Thomas Hale, Sr." Accessed at: https://documents.theblackvault.com/documents/fbifiles/politicians/thomasboggs-fbi1.pdf
"Transcript Concerning the Incident Involving Alaska Airlines 53 on January 30, 1987." Accessed at: https://documents.theblackvault.com/documents/ufos/jal1628/733667-001-030.pdf

Britt, Robert Roy. "First Artificial Neon Sky Show Created." *LiveScience.* Accessed at: https://www.livescience.com/124-artificial-neon-sky-show-created.html

Brocher, T.M., Filson, J.R., Fuis, G.S., Haeussler, P.J., Holzer, T.L., Plafker, G., and Blair, J.L., 2014, The 1964 Great Alaska Earthquake and tsunamis—A modern perspective and enduring legacies: *U.S. Geological Survey Fact Sheet* 2014–3018, 6 p., https://dx.doi.org/10.3133/fs20143018

Brosge, William P., Brabb, Earl E., and King, Elizabeth R. "Geologic Interpretation of Reconnaissance Aeromagnetic Survey of Northeastern Alaska. *The Great State of Alaska Department of Natural Resources*. Accessed at: https://dggs.alaska.gov/webpubs/usgs/b/text/b1271f.pdf

Cecco, Leyland. "Greta Thunberg, Time Traveler?" *The Guardian*. Accessed at: https://www.theguardian.com/environment/2019/nov/22/greta-thunberg-time-traveller-1891-photo

Chalakoski, Martin. "No Traces Found Today of SS Baychimo." *Vintage News*. Accessed at: https://www.thevintagenews.com/2018/02/05/ss-baychimo/

Christiansen, Scott. "They Really Do Want to Believe." Anchorage Press. Accessed at: https://www.anchoragepress.com/news/they-really-do-want-to-believe-alaskas-enduring-place-in-the-literature-of-ufo-sightings/article_e23ef1e8-ec38-52a5-8825-7ecbd731c747.html

Clarke, Jim. "Cargo Jet Lands Safely After Dropping Engine Over Anchorage." *AP News*. Accessed at: https://apnews.com/article/fd11ca29f74027c36f647707836434b4

Coates, Ken and Morrison, Bill. The Sinking of the Princess Sophia. Fairbanks, Alaska: University of Alaska Press, 1991.

Cook Inlet Academy. "Our Founder." Accessed at: https://cookinletacademy.org/staff/our-founder/

Coppock, Mike. "Something's Afoot in Port Chatham." *Alaska Magazine*. Accessed at: https://alaskamagazine.com/authentic-alaska/somethings-afoot-in-port-chatham-century-old-rumors-persist-of-a-terror-in-the-mountains/

Costa, Cheryl. "The USS Williamson UFO Incident." Syracuse Newtimes. Accessed at: https://www.syracusenewtimes.com/the-uss-williamson-ufo-incident/

Cox, Savannah. "The Mysterious Disappearance of the Anjikuni People." *All That's Interesting.* Accessed at: https://allthatsinteresting.com/the-mysterious-disappearance-of-the-anjikuni-people

Demartino, C. and Ricciardelli, F. "Aerodynamics of Nominally Circular Cylinders: A Review of Experimental Results for Civil Engineering Applications." *Engineering Structures.* Accessed at: https://www.sciencedirect.com/topics/earth-and-planetary-sciences/vortex-generator

Dolan, Richard M. *UFOs and the National Security State: Chronology of a Cover-up 1941 – 1973.* Charlottesville, Virginia: Hampton Roads Publishing Company, 2002.

Dunham, Mike. "'Little People' e-mail Zips Through Rural Alaska." *Anchorage Daily News.* Accessed at: https://web.archive.org/web/20110110191605/https://www.adn.com/2008/05/31/422883/little-people-e-mail-zips-through.html

Eberhart, George M. *Mysterious Creatures: A Guide to Cryptozoology, Volume 2.* Santa Barbara, California. ABC-CLIO, Inc., 2002.

Emerging Technology from the arXiv. "Spacecraft Saw ULF Radio Emissions over Haiti before January Quake." *MIT Technology Review.* https://www.technologyreview.com/2010/12/09/89531/spacecraft-saw-ulf-radio-emissions-over-haiti-before-january-quake

Felix, Robert W. "New Study Warns: Magnetic Catastrophe that Wiped Out the Neanderthals is Due to Hit Again." *Climate Science Press.* Accessed at: https://climate-science.press/2021/04/03/magnetic-reversals-far-more-deadly-than-anyone-believed/

Fernando, Christine. "Alaska Earthquake May Have been Most Powerful in US in Half a Century." *USA Today.* Accessed at:

https://www.usatoday.com/story/news/nation/2021/07/29/alask a-earthquake-tsunami-watch-issued-hawaii/5412396001/

FrightFind. "Hotel Captain Cook." Accessed at: https://frightfind.com/hotel-captain-cook/

Frost, Cassandra. "Remote Viewing Underground UFO Bases." *Rense*. Accessed at: https://rense.com/general68/remm.htm

Gearin, Conor. "American's Last Mammoths Died of Thirst on an Alaskan Island." *New Scientist*. Accessed at: https://www.newscientist.com/article/2099485-americas-last-mammoths-died-of-thirst-on-an-alaskan-island/

Gorman, James. "The Explorers Club Once Served Mammoth at a Meal. Or Did It?" The New York Times. Accessed at: https://www.nytimes.com/2016/02/04/science/explorers-club-mammoth-dinner.html

Goyer, Isabel. "After the Accident: 1972 Cessna 310C Alaska Disappearance." *Plane & Pilot*. Accessed at: https://www.planeandpilotmag.com/news/pilot-talk/2020/09/21/1972-cessna-310c-alaska-disappearance/

Greshko, Michael. "DNA Reveals Mysterious Human Cousin With Huge Teeth." *National Geographic*. Accessed at: https://www.nationalgeographic.com/culture/article/151116-denisovan-human-anthropology-ancient-dna

Hancock, Graham. *America Before: The Key To Earth's Lost Civilization*. New York, New York: St. Martin's Press, 2019.

Harrison, Timothy. "Mysterious Alaskan Disappearance." *Lighthouse Digest*. Mar/Apr 2015. Accessed at: http://www.lighthousedigest.com/Digest/StoryPage.cfm?Story Key=4270

"Haunted Alaska: 5 Classic Ghosts Stories." *Anchorage Daily News*. Accessed at: https://www.adn.com/features/article/

notoriously-haunted-alaska-places/2012/10/29/

Haunted Rooms. "The Ghosts of Red Onion Saloon." Accessed at: https://www.hauntedrooms.com/alaska/haunted-places/red-onion-saloon-skagway

Harvey, Ian. "The Mystery of the Octavius." *The Vintage News.* Accessed at: https://www.thevintagenews.com/2016/10/30/the-mystery-of-the-octavius-an-18th-century-ghost-ship-was-discovered-with-the-captains-body-found-frozen-at-his-desk-still-holding-his-pen/

Hollander, Zaz. "Missing Pilot Has Years of Flying Experience." *Anchorage Daily News.* https://www.adn.com/alaska-news/article/missing-pilot-has-years-flying-experience/2013/09/17/

Holmes, Loren. "HAARP Opens its Doors to the Public." *Anchorage Daily News.* Accessed at: https://www.adn.com/alaska-news/science/2018/08/26/haarp-opens-its-doors-to-the-public-but-some-minds-prove-hard-to-change/

Hylton, Wil S. "The Gospel According to Jimmy." *GQ.* Accessed at: https://www.gq.com/story/jimmy-carter-ted-kennedy-ufo-republicans

Hunt, Katie. "Scientists Want to Resurrect the Woolly Mammoth." CNN. Accessed at: https://www.cnn.com/2021/09/13/world/woolly-mammoth-resurrect-deextinction-scn/index.html

Iati, Marisa. "A plane carrying Cokie Roberts's father disappeared over Alaska. He was never found." The Washington Post. Accessed at: https://www.washingtonpost.com/history/2019/09/17/plane-carrying-cokie-robertss-father-disappeared-over-alaska-he-was-never-found/

Kazingnuk, Michael Francis. *The Eskimo History Story.* Alaska State Library. Accessed at: https://library.alaska.gov/hist/hist_docs/docs/asl_MS_197.pdf

Keel, John. *Our Haunted Planet*. Monee, Illinois: Fawcett Publications, 1971.

KINY Radio. "Mysteries of Portlock Alaska and the Abandonment of the Small Town in the 1900s." Accessed at: https://www.kinyradio.com/news/news-of-the-north/mysteries-of-portlock-alaska-and-the-abandonment-of-the-small-town-in-the-1900s/

Levi, Steven. *The Clara Nevada: Gold, Greed, Murder, and Alaska's Inside Passage*. Charleston, South Carolina: The History Channel, 2011.

Lighthouse Friends. "Eldred Rock Lighthouse." Accessed at: https://www.lighthousefriends.com/light.asp?ID=828

Maritime History Project, The. "SS Clara Nevada." Accessed at: https://www.maritimeheritage.org/ships/SS-Clara-Nevada.html

Medred, Craig. "Alaska: The Land of Disappearance." *Anchorage Daily News*. Accessed at: https://www.adn.com/uncategorized/article/alaska-land-disappearance/2010/09/09/

Metallic Minerals. "Dominion Creek Alluvial Royalty." Accessed at: https://www.metallic-minerals.com/projects/klondike-gold-district/dominion-creek-alluvial-royalty/

Meyer, David. "Ghost Ship: Tracking Down the Octavius Legend." Accessed at: http://www.davidmeyercreations.com/mysteries-of-history/ghost-ship-the-octavius-legend/

Miller, Joshua Rhett and Greenstreet, Steven. "Classified 'brief': Secret UFO Report Only 17 Pages Long." *New York Post*. Accessed at: https://nypost.com/2021/07/16/classified-brief-secret-ufo-report-only-17-pages-long/

Milner, Terry. "The Very Strange Death of Top Remote Viewer Pat Price." *Rense*. Accessed at: https://rense.com//general9/stranged.htm

Mind Control: HAARP & The Future of Technology. Directed by Bryan Law, Reality Entertainment, 2017.

Mondor, Colleen. "Missing In Alaska." *Plane & Pilot.* Accessed at: https://www.planeandpilotmag.com/article/missing-in-alaska/

Mondor, Colleen. "Planes Gone Missing Without a Trace Dot Alaska's Aviation History." *Anchorage Daily News.* Accessed at: https://www.adn.com/bush-pilot/article/look-history-missing-aircraft- alaska/2014/03/29/

Moore, Lansing. "Once Frozen in Ice, Now Frozen in Time: Artifacts of an Arctic Voyage." *New York Botanical Garden.* Accessed at: https://www.nybg.org/blogs/science-talk/2016/09/once-frozen-in-ice-now-frozen-in-time-artifacts-of-an-arctic-voyage/

National Oceanic and Atmospheric Administration. "Alaska ShoreZone: Mapping Over 46,000 Miles of Coastal Habitat." Accessed at: https://response.restoration.noaa.gov/about/media/alaska-shorezone-mapping-over-46000-miles-coastal-habitat.html

National UFO Reporting Center. "Balls of Light Seen From Cruise Ship in Alaska." Accessed at: http://nuforc.org/webreports/046/S46283.html
"Fort Greely UFO Sighting." Accessed at: http://www.nuforc.org/webreports/138/ S138315.html
"Prince William Sound, AK." Accessed at: http://nuforc.org/webreports/092/S92477.html

Nelson, Dustin. "Researchers Say 'Upside Down Cosmic Ray Shower' May Be Evidence of a Parallel Universe." *Thrillist.* Accessed at: https://www.thrillist.com/news/nation/nasa-detects-parallel-universe-antarctica-cosmic-ray-shower

Oberhaus, Daniel. "The Hunt Is On For Elusive Ghost Particles in

Antarctica. *Wired.* Accessed at: https://www.wired.com/story/the-hunt-is-on-for-elusive-ghost-particles-in-antarctica/

Office of the Director of National Intelligence. "Preliminary Assessment: Unidentified Aerial Phenomena." Accessed at: https://www.dni.gov/files/ODNI/documents/assessments/Prelimary-Assessment-UAP-20210625.pdf

Pappas, Stephanie. "Conspiracy Theories Abound as U.S. Military Closes HAARP." *LiveScience.* Accessed at: https://www.nbcnews.com/ science/weird-science/conspiracy-theories-abound-u-s-military-closes-haarp-n112576

"Pilots Sighting in Alaska, August 4, 1947." Accessed at: https://ufologie.patrickgross.org/bb/peckdaly1947.htm

Price, Michael. "Ancient DNA Puts a Face on the Mysterious Denisovans." *Science.* Accessed at: https://www.science.org/news/2019/09/ancient-dna-puts-face-mysterious-denisovans-extinct-cousins-neanderthals

Resneck, Jacob. "The Haunting of Alaskan Hotel's Room 315." *Alaska Public Media.* Accessed: https://www.alaskapublic.org /2018/10/26/ak-the-haunting-of-alaskan-hotels-room-315/

Roos, Dave. "'Broken Arrow': When the First U.S. Atomic Bomb Went Missing." *History.* Accessed at: https://www.history.com /news/broken-arrow-first-lost-nuke-canada

Rozell, Ned. "When the Gobi Desert Visited Alaska." University of Alaska Fairbanks. Accessed at: https://www.gi.alaska.edu/ alaska-science-forum/when-gobi-desert-visited-alaska

Schandelmeier, John. "Tales of Lake Iliamna Monster Resurface With New Sightings." Anchorage Daily News. Accessed at: https://www.adn.com/outdoors-adventure/2017/06/28/lake-illiamna-monster-lore-resurfaces-with-new-sightings/#

Schnabel, Jim. *Remote Viewers: The Secret History of America's*

Psychic Spies. New York, New York: Dell Publishing, 1997.

Shabad, Theodore. "Letter in Bottle Recalls Lost Chapter in Arctic Exploration." *The New York Times*. Accessed at: https://www.nytimes.com/1981/04/06/world/letter-in-bottle-recalls-lost-chapter-in-arctic-exploration.html

Silva, Freddy. *The Divine Blueprint: Temples, Power Places and the Global Plan to Shape the Human Soul*. Portland, Maine: Invisible Temple, 2016.

Simkin, John. "Thomas Hale Boggs." *Spartacus Educational*. Accessed at: https://spartacus-educational.com/JFKboggs.htm

Smith, Darren. "Framing Nantiinaq: Alaska's Best KnownCryptid Homicide Case Debunked." *Anchorage Press*. Accessed at: https://www.anchoragepress.com/news/framing-nantiinaq-alaska-s-best-known-cryptid-homicide-case-debunked/article_ed6facfe-a1f9-11eb-b7fc-0bba856ee2fe.html

Sportsman Blog. "Timeline History of the Iliamna Lake Monster." Accessed at: https://www.fishasl.com/timeline-history-lake-iliamna-monster/

Tel-Aviv University. "Unlocking the Secrets of Earth's Magnetic Field From 9,000-Year-Old Recordings." Accessed at: https://scitechdaily.com/unlocking-the-secrets-of-earths-magnetic-field-from-9000-year-old-recordings/

Third Eye Spies. Directed by Lance Mungia, Conscious Universe Films, 2019.

Vernon, Katie. "The Wandering Ghost Ship." *The Vintage News*. Accessed at: https://www.thevintagenews.com/2018/09/11/ss-baychimo-ghost-ship/

Vieira, Jim and Newman, Hugh. *Giants on Record: America's Hidden History, Secrets in the Mounds and the Smithsonian Files*. Glastonbury, Somerset, UK: Avalon Rising Productions,

2015.

Schnabel, Jim. *Remote Viewers: The Secret History of America's Psychic Spies*. New York, New York: Dell Publishing, 1997.

Voosen, Paul. "Ancient Kauri Trees Capture Last Collapse of Earth's Magnetic Field." *Science*. Accessed at: https://www.science.org/news/2021/02/ancient-kauri-trees-capture-last-collapse-earth-s-magnetic-field

Weatherly, David. *Monsters of the Last Frontier*. Nevada: Eerie Lights, 2020.

Weisberger, Mindy. "Chain of Alaskan Islands Might Really Be One Monster Volcano." Live Science. Accessed at: https://www.livescience.com/small-islands-one-big-volcano.html

Weiss, Lawrence D. "Unfriendly Skies: The Extraordinary Story of Flight JAL 1628." *Anchorage Press*. Accessed at: https://www.anchoragepress.com/news/unfriendly-skies-the-extraordinary-flight-of-jal-alaska-s-best/article_8e2d3270-f9d5-11e9-b9db-7ba9229138ae.html

Wilson, Tracy V. "Why Does the North Pole Move?" *How Stuff Works*. Accessed at: https://science.howstuffworks.com/environmental/earth/geophysics/question782.htm

Zell, Holly. "Earth's Atmospheric Layers." NASA. Accessed at: https://www.nasa.gov/mission_pages/sunearth/science/atmosphere-layers2.html

INDEX

ABOUT THE AUTHOR

Mike Ricksecker is the author of the Amazon best-selling *A Walk In The Shadows: A Complete Guide To Shadow People* and the historic paranormal books *Ghosts of Maryland, Ghosts and Legends of Oklahoma, Campfire Tales: Midwest, Ghostorian Case Files*, and the *Encounters With The Paranormal* series. He has appeared on multiple television shows and programs as a paranormal historian, including Travel Channel's *The Alaska Triangle*, Discovery+'s *Fright Club*, Animal Planet's *The Haunted*, Bio Channel's *My Ghost Story*, and RenTV's (Russia) *Mysteries of Mankind*. Mike also produces his own Internet supernatural-based shows on the Haunted Road Media YouTube channel, and is the producer and director of the docu-series, *The Shadow Dimension*, available on several streaming platforms.

On Tuesday and Wednesday nights, he hosts *The Edge of the Rabbit Hole* livestream show and the *Connecting the Universe* interactive class, respectively. Haunted Road Media is also his own paranormal and supernatural book publishing and video production company representing a number of paranormal authors, winning the award for Excellent Media In The Paranormal Field at the 2019 Shockfest Film Festival.

Mike's historic paranormal articles have been published in *The Baltimore Sun, Paranormal Underground Magazine*, and he previously wrote an Oklahoma City paranormal column for Examiner.com (2010 – 2014). His work has also been featured in *The Oklahoman, The Frederick News Post*, Marshall University's *The Parthenon*, and Louisiana State University's *Civil War Book Review*. He now hosts many of these articles along with informational videos and learnings courses on the Connected Universe Portal website.

A native of Cleveland, Ohio, Mike is a father of four and is an avid baseball fan.

Other Haunted Road Media titles from Mike Ricksecker:

A WALK IN THE SHADOWS

Shadow people are some of the most mysterious entities in the known universe, and Mike Ricksecker has experienced many, starting with a tall, dark humanoid figure that appeared in his room as a child. A Walk In The Shadows explores the secrets of the dark while unveiling an enigmatic world feared by many and misunderstood by most.

GHOSTORIAN CASE FILES

Crack open the case files of a Ghostorian and venture into the depths of mysterious historic paranormal investigations! Unlock hidden secrets through exhibits of collected supernatural evidence and carefully researched data, connecting dots that have been centuries in the making.

DEADLY HEIRS

Saying Earl Kiddering is rich is like saying Babe Ruth hit a couple of home runs, but saying he's dead is more accurate. A month after the billionaire drowns in his own swimming pool, Earl's great-niece hires private investigator Chase Michael DeBarlo to find Kiddering's missing will while other family members squabble over the fortune. Deadly Heirs explores the loyalties (and disloyalties) of family bonds.

ENCOUNTERS WITH THE PARANORMAL

Almost everyone has a ghost story. Real people. Real stories. Read about haunted houses and vehicles, experiences during paranormal investigations, visits from relatives that have passed on, pets reacting to the paranormal, psychic experiences, and conversations with full-bodied apparitions. ENCOUNTERS WITH THE PARANORMAL reveals personal stories of the supernatural, exploring the realm beyond the veil.

ENCOUNTERS WITH THE PARANORMAL, Vol. 2

In this second volume, read about more haunted houses, visits from relatives who have passed on, messages from pets from the other side, experiences during paranormal investigations, psychic experiences, hauntings by shadow people, including a dedicated section to the historic Goldenrod Showboat. ENCOUNTERS WITH THE PARANORMAL: Volume 2 reveals more personal stories of the supernatural, continuing to explore the realm beyond the veil.

ENCOUNTERS WITH THE PARANORMAL, Vol. 3

In this third volume, read about more haunted houses, supernatural creatures, messages from pets from the other side, haunted history, experiences during paranormal investigations, psychic experiences, and more, including a dedicated section to the historic Mineral Springs Hotel. ENCOUNTERS WITH THE PARANORMAL: VOLUME 3 reveals more personal stories of the supernatural and paranormal, continuing to explore the realm beyond the veil through its contributors.

ENCOUNTERS WITH THE PARANORMAL, Vol. 4

Volume four of the ENCOUNTERS WITH THE PARANORMAL series covers even more haunted houses, supernatural creatures, experiences during paranormal investigations, haunted history, and psychic experiences than any of its predecessors. You are not alone! This offering also includes a dedicated section to the historic Ferry Plantation and its many haunts.

Haunted Road Media
www.hauntedroadmedia.com

Join us at the Connected Universe Portal:
www.connecteduniverseportal.com

Made in the USA
Monee, IL
11 November 2021